RESPO... TO SUICIDE

"Priests, deacons, lay pastoral ministers, counselors, and those preparing for ministry will find in this thoughtful collection both sure guidance and practical wisdom as they accompany others in navigating the painful experience of suicide and the many complex questions—existential, theological, moral, and spiritual—it raises."

Msgr. Michael Heintz
Seminary Academic Dean
Mount St. Mary's University
Emmitsburg, Maryland

"*Responding to Suicide* is a rich and compelling resource for Catholic ministerial leaders and for those preparing for ministry! Articles include clinical guidelines for assessment, treatment, and prevention of suicide; historical and contemporary insights into Church teaching; suicide prevention competencies; and wise and compassionate approaches to accompaniment of those who suffer from pervasive psychological pain, as well as those who suffer as survivors of suicide loss. Finally, it is the kind of sound, nuanced, and non-judgmental resource so many Catholic leaders have sought for years. A must-read for those exercising or preparing for ministry!"

Jan Poorman
Director of Formation and Field Education
Master of Divinity Program
University of Notre Dame

"Every parish needs this enormously helpful book, because at some point every pastoral leader will need to respond to a suicide. The heartfelt stories from families affected by suicide, accompanied by accurate medical data and authentic theological direction, provide a clear, comprehensive, and profoundly practical guide for all your parish ministers."

Fr. Dave Heney
Pastor
St. Bruno Catholic Church
Whittier, California

"The mother of a young man who died by suicide shared with me her conviction that the effects of suicide are contagious. Not only is a loved one lost, but far too often family and friends are plunged into a grief that is accompanied by unnecessary shame and guilt. This much-needed book is a great help for those who cry, 'Why, O Lord?'"

Cardinal Timothy Dolan
Archbishop of New York

"A beautiful blending of the personal and the pastoral, *Responding to Suicide* is a revelation—and something the Church has needed for a long time. Deacon Ed Shoener has taken his own grief and transformed it into a moving and consoling gift that will benefit Catholics everywhere who have lost a loved one to suicide. The contributors of this powerful book teach pastoral leaders how to offer insight, compassion, consolation, and hope."

Deacon Greg Kandra
Journalist and blogger at *The Deacon's Bench*

"*Responding to Suicide* is a fantastic book and great gift to the Catholic Church. This is a valuable and practical resource for anyone serving in ministry. Led by personal testimony from Catholic leaders, this book dispels the stigma of suicide on a pastoral level and advances this necessary discussion with clarity, humility, and courage."

Scott Weeman
Founder and executive director of Catholic in Recovery

"*Responding to Suicide* is a powerful book. The authors provide practical and faithful guidance to those who will work with people touched by suicide. In direct and compassionate language, the stories told in the book will shape our response, making us more empathetic and helpful. I have faced suicide personally and professionally. This book would have helped me then, and I'm so very glad it is available now."

Kathy Mears
Chief Program Officer
National Catholic Educational Association

"*Responding to Suicide* is, to say the least, urgently needed. As deaths by suicide increase, we Catholic leaders must equip ourselves with compassionate truth instead of pastorally inadequate and too-often inaccurate words and gestures. So much misunderstanding surrounds Catholics and suicide, which is precisely why this book is not just very good but also essential for those of us charged with the pastoral care of God's people."

Fr. Joshua J. Whitfield
Pastoral Administrator
St. Rita Catholic Community and School
Dallas, Texas

"Our country loses an estimated twenty veterans a day to suicide. It's not enough to feel terrible about this tragic situation; we must try to do what we can to help our fellow human beings who are in crisis. Help and resources are available. This book provides urgently needed information and practical guidance. I highly recommend it. Please help."

Bishop Joseph L. Coffey
Vicar for Veterans Affairs
Archdiocese for the Military Services, USA

RESPONDING
TO
SUICIDE

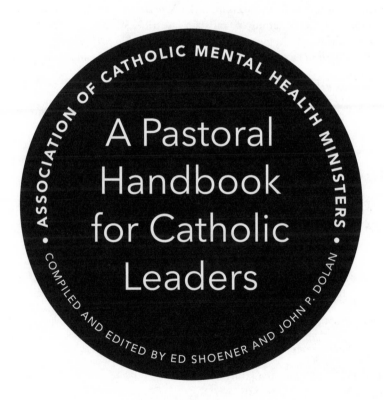

ASSOCIATION OF CATHOLIC MENTAL HEALTH MINISTERS

A Pastoral
Handbook
for Catholic
Leaders

COMPILED AND EDITED BY ED SHOENER AND JOHN P. DOLAN

AVE MARIA PRESS AVE Notre Dame, Indiana

Nihil Obstat: Rev. Royce V. Gregerson, S.T.L.
　　　　　　Censor deputatus
Imprimatur　Most Reverend Kevin C. Rhoades
　　　　　　Bishop of Fort Wayne–South Bend
　　　　　　August 28, 2020

Foreword © 2020 by Kevin W. Vann, J.C.D., D.D.

Founded in 1865, Ave Maria Press is a ministry of the United States Province of Holy Cross.

www.avemariapress.com

Paperback: ISBN-13 978-1-64680-011-7
E-book: ISBN-13 978-1-64680-012-4

Cover image © yokeetod / iStock / Getty Images Plus.
Cover and text design by Samantha Watson.
Printed and bound in the United States of America.

Library of Congress Cataloging-in-Publication Data is available.

Contents

Foreword

Forty years ago this month I was ordained a transitional deacon at the Cathedral of the Immaculate Conception in Springfield, Illinois. The next month, in June of 1980, I was assigned to serve at the very same parish. Having grown up in Springfield, I knew the place well and was blessed to have as my first pastor there Fr. Charles Mulcrone, who has a most kind, patient, and pastoral example of priestly ministry. The very first week, Fr. Mulcrone assigned me the task of presiding and preaching at a funeral of someone who had died by suicide. I did not know the family, but I relied on Mulcrone's experience and also that of my mother, who was a nurse at St. John's Hospital in Springfield, and on my own experience working as a medical technologist. I do not remember my homily at this distance of forty years, but I kept up with the family for a while and remember their gratitude for the time that I spent with them. I remember as well that same summer how I answered the door of the rectory to encounter an individual with bipolar disorder in obvious confusion and distress. I walked with that person for hours up and down Fifth Street listening and trying to bring some calm. Instinctively, I let this individual talk as we walked and I suggested that we pray the Rosary. That seemed to help.

In the years that followed, from Springfield to Fort Worth, Texas, to here in Orange, California, I have been blessed to walk with other families, parish communities, and church personnel accompany in faith many who struggle through the challenges of mental illness and suicide loss. All of these experiences became for me stepping stones in learning more and learning how to pray through the challenges that these tragedies bring to so many. God's providence has been at work in my life.

I think of my friendship with Pastor Rick and Kay Warren here in Orange, California and how together, after the suicide of their son Matthew, we worked so that the Diocese of Orange and Saddleback Church could help. We learned to walk with families in those moments and help them find paths toward healing. More recently, I have been able to be a part of the "Whole Person Care" initiative here in the State of California, which has sought to expand the notion of care for those in need, in their experiences of illness, suffering, and pain, in our parishes and institutions.

I was blessed to have been guided by God's providence in all of those steps. And now, we are once again wonderfully blessed to have the steps toward healing clearly set in front of us in *Responding to Suicide: A Pastoral Handbook for Catholic Leaders*—the work of Deacon Ed Shoener and my good friend Bishop John P. Dolan of San Diego along with a dozen other contributors. With the wisdom, experience, and faith of the authors of each chapter, some of whom I know well, we who lead and pastor the Church will be better prepared to comfort, console, and companion those who come into our lives wounded by the pain of mental illness and suicide. They come to us never by chance but, I believe, by the hand of God!

I want to close this reflection with the words of Fr. Jonathon Raia, which beautifully sums up the pastoral reflections in this book, and are certainly appropriate in the closing weeks of this Paschal season: "Jesus came so that you and I would know that love. And even through his Church, Jesus wants to give us the strength in every moment with the hope that only comes from knowing that Jesus has risen from the dead, and that light shines in darkness, and the darkness had not overcome it."

Most Rev. Kevin W. Vann J.C.D., D.D.
Bishop of Orange in California
Vice President of the California Catholic Conference
May 18, 2020

Introduction

SUICIDE AND THE NEED FOR THE HEALING PRESENCE OF CHRIST

Deacon Ed Shoener
Diocese of Scranton

Suicide is a common way to die. According to the National Institutes of Health, on a typical day in the United States, more than 130 people will die from suicide. In the United States, it is a leading cause of death, claiming more than forty-eight thousand people each year. Shockingly, it is the second leading cause of death among young people between the ages of ten and thirty-four, with about 15,000 people in this demographic dying per year. It is a global tragedy, with the World Health Organization reporting more than 850,000 people dying worldwide from suicide every year. Suicide is an anguishing and persistent cause of death.

By its nature, death by suicide is sudden, often violent, and often comes at the end of a long and difficult struggle with mental illness. Heaped on top of that is the social stigma that comes with both mental illness and suicide. As a result, families who lose a loved one to suicide are very often left in shock and intensely burdened with shame. This is a fierce suffering that cries out for the healing presence of Christ, his Church, and his ministers.

The purpose of this book is to respond to those cries by providing spiritual insights and resources for those who are grieving a suicide death as well as sound and authoritative pastoral guidance for those who are ministering to them.

Since my daughter, Katie, died by suicide in 2016, I have ministered to many Catholics who are grieving the death of a loved one by suicide. I have come to realize that these people long for spiritual support from the Church. Yet many tell me that, beyond making the necessary funeral arrangements, they have never spoken to a member of the clergy about their loved one's death by suicide. When I ask why these people are reluctant to talk to their parish priest or deacon, I regularly hear three disheartening concerns:

1. They doubt that clergy and other Church leaders understand their experience.
2. They fear that the Church teaches their loved one is probably in hell.
3. They see nowhere to find support in the Catholic Church.

Let's take each of those concerns and consider why they exist and what can be done to address them.

FIRST CONCERN OF THOSE WHO GRIEVE

Doubt That Clergy and Other Catholic Leaders Understand

The first step in assuring people that members of the clergy and other Catholic leaders understand suicide is for these leaders to educate themselves on the topic and to learn how to openly talk about suicide and mental illness. Although there are some who have developed the ability to minister with great compassion and understanding when there is a suicide death, far too many are not adequately prepared to minister to those who are grieving the death a loved one from suicide. That needs to change.

Misunderstanding is widespread and stories about the lack of understanding abound. All too often Catholic leaders and clergy simply shake their head in bewilderment when they hear that a young person who was married and had children, a good job, and a fine life died by suicide. They ignore or are silent when someone makes gross and inappropriate gestures that imitate and mock death by suicide. When the death of someone by suicide comes up in conversation there is no open and empathetic discussion about how best to minister to the person's family and help them heal.

Some priests even claim that they have never presided at the funeral of someone who died by suicide. Statistically, that claim is awfully hard to accept, which begs the question, why would a priest not be told by their parishioners that a love one has died by suicide? Where has this lack of trust or confidence in the support of the Church come from?

There has been much commentary recently over the rise in suicide rates in the United States. Unfortunately, and mistakenly, some religious commentators have suggested that this is because of what they perceive as a decline in the morality and religiosity of the culture. They suggest that if our culture returned to the higher moral standards and religious values that existed in the past, then the current suicide rate would be lower. However, this assertion is based on assumptions wholly unsupported by historical suicide data.

Statistical data show us that while suicide rates have fluctuated during the past hundred years in the United States, there has been no significant change in the overall average rate of suicide. Professor Matthew K. Nock, the director of the Nock Lab at Harvard's Department of Psychology, researches suicide and self-injury. In a 2016 article, he wrote, "In 2014, the suicide rate was 13 per 100,000 people. In 1914, the rate was 16 per 100,000. So, the suicide rate now is about the same as it was 100 years ago. I would interpret this not that it isn't a problem, but that [it] has always been a problem. For the past 100 years, despite treatments and research efforts, the suicide rate remains extremely high."[1]

In a *New York Times* op-ed article, Richard A. Friedman, a professor of clinical psychiatry and the director of the psychopharmacology clinic at the Weill Cornell Medical College stated,

> We have seen the rates of death from heart disease and HIV plummet over time. Not so for suicide. The simple reason suicide has been neglected for so long is stigma. It is a human behavior that terrifies most people. Suicide is wrongly seen as a character or moral flaw—or even a sinful act. It is viewed as something shameful that must be hidden. But suicide is a medical problem that is almost always associated with several common and treatable mental illnesses, like depression and anxiety, along with impulse and substance abuse disorders. It is estimated that more than 90 percent of those who die by suicide have a diagnosable mental disorder.[2]

Friedman goes on to state, "We need to talk more openly about suicide, to help people see it as the treatable medical scourge that it is." His conclusion is that "we should declare war on suicide—just as we've done with other public health threats like HIV and heart disease—and give it the research and clinical funding needed to beat it."[3]

Mental illnesses, which are the root cause of many suicides, are neither caused nor cured by religious faith or moral values of patients. The number of suicides will be reduced once there is better care and treatment for mental illness and suicidality.

All too often people who are having suicidal thoughts feel ashamed that they are thinking of suicide and will not talk about it. Having suicidal thoughts is like having chest pains if you have a heart condition; it is a critical medical warning sign, not a moral failing or a character flaw, and a person needs to get the proper care as soon as possible. We need to be compassionate and be able to talk to them about their suicidal thoughts and direct them to a suicide helpline, a mental health professional, or a hospital. We can pray with them to find the strength and support to get them the care they need. But we need to be clear—prayer by itself will not cure mental illness.

Rather than understanding suicide primarily as a medical problem, all too often within the Church it gets mixed into theological discussions about euthanasia. There are false equivalencies in doing so that must be addressed.

Euthanasia is undertaken when a person has a terminal illness and is seeking to avoid the suffering that will come with it. The problem with talking about suicide within the context of a discussion about euthanasia is that it perpetuates one of the long-standing mistaken beliefs about suicide: that it is a rational act. Euthanasia is different than suicide because it is fully considered and openly discussed for a period time and the drugs are quietly administered by a medical professional. Euthanasia is morally wrong, but it is considered in a deliberate and rational manner.

In contrast, suicide is self-inflicted, often violent and impulsive, ugly, and usually rooted in the irrational despair of a mental illness. Suicide is all too often how a mental illness terminates. In this way, suicide often functions as organ failure does with other illnesses such as diabetes or multiple sclerosis: it is often the end of a long illness. An impulsive suicide in response to a significant stressor, such as a job loss or a criminal charge, is like a sudden death from an aneurism or cardiac arrest.

If Catholic clergy and other leaders are going to be known as people who understand suicide, then they must be able to assure people that they have a basic understanding of mental illness and suicide, particularly that suicide is usually associated with a serious chronic or acute mental illness and often caused by the illness. Suicide has to do with different individual thresholds for enduring psychological pain and the causes are unique to each person.

People grieving a suicide need to know that Catholic leaders will not be making theological judgments about their loved one or suggesting that the suicide was the result of a poor moral choice or a character flaw. Only God knows the state of a soul at the moment of death, whether it is from suicide or another cause.

We need to get out of the habit of using the phrase "committed suicide." It is loaded with judgment, and Catholic leaders should stop using it. Instead use phrases such as "died by suicide" or "took his own life." Criminals commit crimes, but a death from suicide is not a crime. We all commit sins, but only God can judge if a suicide was a sinful turning away from God or if it was a desperate act rooted in deep and irrational pain that cried out for God's mercy. Using phrases such as "died from suicide" can help shift how we talk and think about suicide from a place of judgment to a healthier place where there can be discussion about mental illness and the real causes of suicide. This in turn will encourage better treatment programs for those we know to be at risk for suicide and more compassionate pastoral care of those who lose a loved one to suicide.

I have never heard a regular Sunday homily that touched on suicide and mental illness, and I am certain my experience is common. Since Katie's death, I occasionally talk about mental illness and suicide in homilies. When I do, many people make a point to tell me that it was the first time they ever heard these topics mentioned in a homily. This same lack of attention pertains to the Universal Prayer or the intercessions offered at Mass. These prayers are offered for all kinds of issues and problems, but how often are they offered for those who are living with mental illness such as schizophrenia, bipolar disorder, or clinical depression or for those who are self-harming or contemplating suicide? Tragically, in most churches the answer is *never*.

Catholic leaders need to be able to compassionately talk about suicide and not be afraid to be open about their own personal experience of suicide in their lives and ministry. It has been my experience that some members of the clergy can be reluctant to talk about familial suicide because they are concerned that it may affect how people relate to them and that somehow they will be diminished in the eyes of their parishioners. But these attitudes just add to the stigma and shame that grieving families experience.

Before clergy can appropriately offer pastoral care and guidance when responding to suicide, they need to find the courage and words to talk about their own personal experiences of it, whether they have lost a loved one to suicide or have come to know about suicide through the wealth of information medical science has to offer. To address this concern, the first section of this book is a small collection of essays from Catholic leaders sharing spiritual insights they have gained after a family member or other loved one died by suicide. Catholic leaders can lead the way in bringing the healing balm of Christ's love into the lives of people who are grieving the death of a loved one by suicide simply by learning to talk openly about mental illness and suicide.

SECOND CONCERN OF THOSE WHO GRIEVE

Fear That the Church Teaches Their Loved One Is Probably in Hell

Many years ago, I occasionally visited a man who lived alone to check in on him and to give him some company. As I got to know this man, he talked about his wife and how he kissed her good night every evening. She had died by suicide more than thirty years earlier, and he was kissing the urn that held her cremains. My friend still grieved deeply because when his wife died, the Church would not allow a funeral Mass for her and would not allow her to be buried in the family burial plot at the local Catholic cemetery. Because the Church did not take care of him and his wife when she died, he was doing the best he could to care for her.

After speaking about mental illness and suicide at a parish event, a person came up to me in tears to talk about their father's death by suicide, which had occurred more than forty years earlier. This person told me that day was the first time they felt free to talk about it at a Church event. For more than forty years, this person had held their grief, with no direct support from the Church.

Stories like these are not unusual. The history of how the Church as an institution has, for the most part, responded to suicide has resulted far too often in stifling unresolved grief, deep shame, often crippling spiritual wounds, and psychological damage that never heals.

Within living memory and well into the twentieth century, the Church denied a funeral Mass to people who died by suicide and would not allow them to be buried in a Catholic cemetery. A person who died by suicide was understood to have died in a state of mortal sin, and the teaching of the Church is that mortal sin "causes exclusion from Christ's kingdom and the eternal death of hell" (*CCC*, 1861). Although the Church has never directly said that any individual is in fact in hell and asserts that we must "entrust the judgment of persons to the justice and mercy of God" (*CCC*, 1861), this basic teaching on mortal sin was used to justify denying a funeral Mass and burial in a Catholic cemetery for people who died by suicide.

Fortunately, as our understanding of psychology broadly and mental illness particularly has improved, the Church has developed a more nuanced and compassionate teaching on suicide. But the effects of the Church's history persist and continue to do harm. In an effort to overcome these wounds, Catholic leaders need to educate people about the Church's current teaching and reassure those who grieve that the Church prays for those who have died by suicide.

In 1992, Pope John Paul II promulgated the *Catechism of the Catholic Church* (*CCC*). The teaching on suicide is short, to the point, and reflects advances in the medical sciences pertaining to mental illness and other psychological dysfunctions. The *Catechism* section on suicide reads as follows:

Suicide

(2280) Everyone is responsible for his life before God who has given it to him. It is God who remains the sovereign Master of life. We are obliged to accept life gratefully and preserve it for his honor and the salvation of our souls. We are stewards, not owners, of the life God has entrusted to us. It is not ours to dispose of.

(2281) Suicide contradicts the natural inclination of the human being to preserve and perpetuate his life. It is gravely contrary to the just love of self. It likewise offends love of neighbor because it unjustly breaks the ties of solidarity with family, nation, and other human societies to which we continue to have obligations. Suicide is contrary to love for the living God.

(2282) If suicide is committed with the intention of setting an example, especially to the young, it also takes on the gravity of scandal. Voluntary co-operation in suicide is contrary to the moral law.

Grave psychological disturbances, anguish, or grave fear of hardship, suffering, or torture can diminish the responsibility of the one committing suicide.

(2283) We should not despair of the eternal salvation of persons who have taken their own lives. By ways known to him alone, God can provide the opportunity for salutary repentance. The Church prays for persons who have taken their own lives.

I have talked to many people who have attempted suicide and every one of them has been glad they survived the attempt. Each of them also agrees with the essential teaching presented in *Catechism* sections 2280 and 2281. They each believe that suicide is wrong. However, they also agree with the third section, 2282, because they know that their suicide attempt was driven by irrational thoughts and psychological disorder. Once these persons were stabilized and able to think more clearly, they did not want to die by suicide. But the effects of mental illness can come back with a vengeance, and statistics clearly show that after a person has attempted suicide once, their risk for dying by suicide sometime later increases significantly.

The final paragraph of the *Catechism* section on suicide, 2283, has brought great comfort to me and to many others who grieve the loss of a loved one by suicide. I do not despair for the eternal salvation of my daughter, Katie. I know that she is loved by God, and I look to Mary and the saints for consolation and help.

In the months before she died, Katie prayed novenas to St. Theresa for help with her mental illness. When my wife, Ruth, and I cleaned out her apartment after she died, we found and have saved a holy card of Pope Francis smiling and giving a hopeful thumbs-up that Katie had in her bedroom. She kept a colorful cross in her room that had these words on it: "Be Strong. Be Courageous." That cross now hangs underneath a picture of Katie in our home.

The funeral Mass for Katie was beautiful and was attended by many members of the clergy, including our bishop. She is buried at the Cathedral Cemetery in her hometown of Scranton, Pennsylvania. We are consoled knowing that the Church prays for Katie.

The best time to discuss the Church's teaching on suicide is before a suicide occurs. It would be helpful for the faithful to hear about this teaching at times other than in the immediate aftermath of a suicide. Occasional reference to this teaching in a Sunday or daily homily, in a bulletin notice or some other venue where the Church teaching is routinely explained is the best way to discuss this teaching, so that when a suicide does occur, people already understand what the Church teaches. They are then better prepared to look to the Church for consolation.

Whether this teaching needs to be discussed at the funeral of someone who died by suicide is questionable and should always be discussed with the family before any decision is made in this regard. Like any sudden death (and suicide is almost always sudden), the family is in shock and in deep grief and simply wants to give their loved one a dignified and holy burial. In 2018, national media attention was focused on a parish in the Detroit area when a family became outraged with their pastor because he focused on Church teaching on suicide at their son's funeral Mass. The family wanted the priest to focus on the good qualities of their son and to preach about hope. Although what the priest said may have been an accurate description of what the Church teaches about suicide, the funeral Mass was not the time and place to present it. A more pastoral homily was needed for that family at that most difficult and fragile time.

A funeral Mass is a time to provide consolation and preach the hope that can be found in the Death and Resurrection of Christ. All other matters are secondary. When a person dies from cancer or any other disease, the cause of death is usually not the topic of the funeral homily; it should be the same with suicide. If the family wants the suicide to be discussed, then a brief summary of Church teaching might be appropriate as part of the broader homily about the hope we can find in Christ. There are examples in the appendix of this book on how to discuss suicide at a funeral, if it is appropriate to do so. However, usually it is best to wait for some time after the funeral and then use this teaching to support grief counseling and the ongoing pastoral care of the family.

The second section of this book presents authoritative essays on the history and teaching of the Catholic Church about suicide. This basic information and the theological reflections that accompany presentation of the teachings can help clear up any misconceptions and fears about what the Church now teaches.

THIRD CONCERN OF THOSE WHO GRIEVE

Lack of Support in the Church for Them

All death is painful, but the grief that comes with suicide is unique because of the stigma associated with mental illness and suicide. Families who are grieving the death of a loved one by suicide often feel alone and shamed. Others, even the closest friends and family members, often do not know what to say to them and what is said is very often not at all helpful and sometimes even hurtful. When those who suffer loss by suicide turn to their parishes for support, they all too often find little to nothing in place to offer the support they need.

This can change. This needs to change. We can do better. Clergy and other leaders must learn how to provide pastoral care for members of the faithful grieving a suicide by learning how to be with them in their pain. We must learn how to guide them and direct them to other people and services that can help them along their long road to healing. So, where to begin?

First and foremost, Catholic pastoral leaders can take extra steps to reach out to those grieving a suicide in a manner specifically suited to the experience. We should not wait for the family and other loved ones to ask for help because many will not, due to the stigma and shame they may be feeling. We need to make an extra, well-informed effort to reach out. For example, when we see a member of a grieving family at the parish, we ought to go out of our way to talk with them. Be direct and ask how they and their family are doing in the aftermath of their loved one's death. Perhaps one or more visits to their home, not just immediately after the death but in the weeks and months afterward, will be welcome. Simply ask, as you would with other instances of sudden death.

Following a suicide, families and other loved ones will often isolate themselves from friends and relatives and from the Church. Many will also back away from God. Christ wants to be with families grieving a suicide, and often it is his clergy that he wants to send to be with these families. Although it may be frightening to enter into this deep grief, it is where Christ wants to be. It is particularly true when a child has died from suicide. We must be willing and able to bring the light of Christ into the darkness of grief brought on by suicide.

Families need to know that they are not alone and that their experience of suicide does not make them freakish. A parent who lost a child to suicide said that their family thinks everyone who drives past their house thinks or even says, "That's the suicide house." Likewise, this parent thinks that when people see them in the store, they think to themselves, "There's the suicide parent" and try to avoid them. This parent feels as though they are the only one who has experienced a death by suicide. Although suicide is a common way to die, we do not talk to one another about it and as a result, families grieving a suicide can feel very alone.

As pastoral leaders, we can help change this by talking about the deaths by suicide that have occurred in our own families when we visit those who are grieving a suicide, so that the grieving family does not feel quite so isolated. If you don't have any close family members or friends who have died by suicide, then ask for help from parishioners who have lost someone. Many people who have experienced the suicide of a loved one are very willing to make visits, help clergy offer pastoral care, and companion others toward healing.

As pastoral leaders, we should also be aware of resources within our wider communities. For example, in the Chicago area, Fr. Charles T. Rubey founded a ministry called Loving Outreach to Survivors of Suicide (LOSS). LOSS ministry publishes a monthly email newsletter that has reflections and insights on living with a suicide loss. Fr. Rubey's chapter in this book discusses the LOSS program in more detail and provides specific ideas on how to accompany families who are grieving a suicide loss.

There are suicide support groups in many areas of the country. The American Foundation for Suicide Prevention (AFSP) website includes a page that lets a person search for a support group in their local community. In addition, parishes in many communities offer grief support groups where the grief that comes with suicide can be openly discussed and healing can be found.

To address the concern that the Church offers no support to those who experience loss by suicide, the third and fourth sections of this book contain information on how to support these individuals and families. The third section is a collection of essays by Catholic psychologists, and they provide insights into the psychology of suicide and how to support those who are grieving the suicide of a loved one. The fourth section includes stories from Catholic leaders who have worked in ministries that support individuals, families, and parish communities. In addition, appendices provide information on services, homilies on the topic of suicide, and additional resources for giving spiritual support.

PART I.

GRIEVING SUICIDE

Personal
Reflections
from Catholic
Leaders

1.

Share Your Story and Be Yourself

A MESSAGE FOR SIBLING SURVIVORS OF SUICIDE LOSS

Bishop John Dolan
Diocese of San Diego

This is a message about losing a sibling through suicide. Although my experience is unique to me, and my surviving siblings have their own stories, there is one common thread that we as Christians all share. Our identity as Christians is the key to finding joy even in the midst of pain after the loss of a loved one through suicide.

It was the first day of my eighth-grade year when we buried my brother Tom. I was thirteen years old. The parish church of St. Mary Magdalene was packed with family, friends, and many of my classmates from the School of the Madeleine. It was a day for prayer and grieving. My brother, Tom Dolan, died in Chino State Prison by his own hand. He hanged himself.

MY FAMILY AND MY BROTHER TOM

Tom and I grew up in a large family; he was number five of nine children and I am number seven. We were a strong Catholic family living among equally large families in our neighborhood and, guided by our parents, we were all rooted in faith and community-oriented.

Tom was a handsome, talented, cheerful young man. He seemed to be self-directed and showed evidence of success in his future. He excelled in sports, especially baseball, wrestling, bowling, and rock climbing. He was an artist. He loved art, playing guitar, and singing. Sadly, he also began to enjoy the party scene, which led him away from his first loves.

Soon after high school, Tom began to be more reclusive, hanging around with just a few of his drug friends. Even as a kid—I was in seventh grade when Tom was nineteen years old—I knew that he was hanging around with the wrong crowd. My parents were especially leery of one friend that Tom had invited to our house. It was clear that this friend, Scott, was going nowhere, and drugs seemed to be his only future path in life. For whatever reason, Tom seemed to lean in that direction as well. I had just returned from a Boy Scout trip when I learned that Tom and Scott were on the run from the law. My mom sat me down and explained what had occurred while I was away.

Apparently Tom and Scott had been drinking and using drugs. Whether on impulse or by plan, they decided to rob the house of our next-door neighbor. That same evening, my parents learned of the incident and attempted to confront Tom and Scott. Unfortunately, Tom held a gun—which belonged to Scott—and urged my parents to step out of the way. Shocked, but grateful that Tom (not Scott) was the one in possession of the gun, my parents stepped aside. My brother and his friend made a run for it and, along the way, managed to rob a store. After a few days, Tom and Scott were picked up, and after a few months Tom landed in Chino State Prison. I do not know what happened to Scott.

We are not entirely sure why Tom had taken such a turn for the worse in his later high school years. It could have been simply hanging around the wrong crowd. It could have been something else. In reality, my oldest brother, Steve, was being treated for mental health–related issues and had been just coming off a long series of drug use himself. Perhaps Tom was also beginning to show signs of mental illness.

After Tom landed in prison, our family went to Chino, California, to pay him a visit. I was elated to see my brother for the first time since before my Boy Scouts trip. He looked cleaned up. He showed true contrition, and he seemed to be mending his ways. My parents were especially happy to know that Tom had been visited by a Catholic priest chaplain. After our visit, Tom and I became pen pals. I looked up to him and truly loved him. I really believed that he was on his way to becoming the brother that I once knew and admired.

TOM'S DEATH AND OUR DEVASTATION

But then the horrible news came that Tom had hanged himself in his cell. What devastation! It did not seem possible! Just prior to his suicide, we were all blessed with the news that Tom's sentence was going to be reduced to just a few years. How could it be that this young man in his late teens could spiral so quickly? How was he able to show such signs of improvement and then allow this to occur?

A number of theories as to why Tom killed himself were floating in my mind. My first thought was that he was killed. But there was no evidence of foul play. Another thought was that he was abused in prison and he just couldn't take it. To this day, I still do not know why he hanged himself. All I know is that we were all devastated. I can still picture the pre-vigil, when my mother stared at Tom's body in the casket. My dad was staring at her as she gently touched Tom's body and began to weep. Then Dad began to cry. Soon all my siblings and I started up. That memory is deeply embedded in me.

I knew that my parents were devastated. I would often hear comments—and sometimes still do—that "my parents are strong, but they must be devastated to lose their child." Both are true. To lose a son is tragic. My parents never got over it. Even to this day, they rarely talk about Tom, unless they refer to happier days when our family was together camping, or singing around the piano, or gathered for evening supper.

BURYING OUR PAIN

My parents were born and raised in rural Iowa. They were unfamiliar with therapy and wary of psychology. They managed to move forward with trust in God and in each other. Outside of our common faith and family ties, counseling was not an option. And so my family buried our pain. We all tried to cope, but the pain would manifest itself in many ways. I witnessed among my siblings a loss of faith, hope, and love exhibited through excessive drinking, depression, and even another suicide. Trying to bottle their pain and sorrow, their lives showed signs of unrest. We were affected each in our own way.

As a thirteen-year-old boy, I was affected deeply by Tom's suicide, and my life took a sudden turn. My coming-of-age years, in which I should have discovered my identity and purpose, were stunted. Because of Tom's suicide I put finding my identity and purpose on hold as I witnessed the devastation in my family, especially in the lives of my parents. Rather than just being me, I began to hold claim to a super-persona that looked like this:

Tom was a rock climber, so I took up rock climbing. Tom was a wrestler, so I took up wresting. Tom was in a bowling league, so I joined a bowling league. In each case, I tried to reach beyond his level. I tried to do everything that Tom did, but even better. Of course, I would not use drugs. My parents deserved better. In a nutshell, I needed to save my parents. I needed to be the defender and savior of my family. Even in my Confirmation year—the same year of my brother's suicide—I knew I needed to be a soldier for Christ. In fact, I selected St. Michael the Archangel—soldier and defender—for my Confirmation name.

During my high school years, as I lived this super-life, I recall my dad telling me more than a few times to just be myself. I brushed it off and continued on my journey to be more than Tom. Not me, John—just more than Tom.

After my junior year in high school, I blew out both of my shoulders in a summer wresting league. This set me into depression. I was excelling in the sport and bonding wonderfully with my teammates. It meant everything to me. When I was told that I could no longer wrestle, I was lost. I thought, "Where do I go now?"

After sitting idle for a while, and without a sense of purpose, I too began to show signs of depression. In my senior year I was falling behind in my assignments and my grades began to slip. I never attempted suicide, but I hoped for death. The only thing that kept me going was the knowledge that my parents did not deserve to lose another son.

Rather than living in this world of depression, I started getting involved in our parish youth group. There I found a new set of friends and I seemed to show some signs of leadership in the group. Even the parish priests took notice of me and began to inquire if I would consider becoming a priest. Of course, becoming a priest would fit well with my need to be a savior for my family. At that time, I never outwardly expressed a desire to be my brother Tom or to be a savior of the family. But, subconsciously, the intent was there.

After graduation from high school I entered St. Francis Seminary on the University of San Diego campus to begin studies for the priesthood. The first time I saw a psychologist was when I entered the seminary. It was a necessary part of the application process and, after only one follow-up meeting to a procedural battery of psychological tests, I was seen fit to enter the seminary. I recall my review including a concern about Tom's suicide and what effect it had on me. That was the only time I met a psychologist individually during my entire college career at St. Francis.

SURVIVING A SECOND SUICIDE

When I was nineteen years old, tragedy hit our family again. We had gathered for Thanksgiving dinner, the table was set, and we were waiting for my sister Therese and her husband, Joe, to arrive. Instead, the police showed up and told us the horrible news that Therese had hanged herself in a local canyon just hours earlier. Then the news got worse. The police officers told us that Joe was expected to tell my parents about my sister's death, but instead he died by suicide, having ended his life by asphyxiation in his car that same morning.

To this day, the particular reason for Therese's suicide is unclear to me. Apparently there was marital hardship. That Joe killed himself hours after Therese died by suicide would seem to back that up. He left his own suicide note for my parents, but I never had the opportunity to read it.

My sister Therese was a few years older than Tom. She was a kind person who had a beautiful smile. She was introverted and talented. Like Tom, she played guitar and was an up-and-coming graphic artist. I used to enjoy spending time in her room drawing and painting alongside her. She would give me tips on drawing faces. I remember her saying, "Begin with the eyes. The eyes express everything!" She excelled in her talents, earning a master's degree from the University of California San Diego and becoming an art instructor at a Catholic school.

Our family knew that Therese's marriage seemed strained from the beginning. I remember thinking that she seemed to be in a rush to have a wedding, but it was her life and she seemed happy. The family never quite took to Joe and, I believe, Therese knew that. Joe was in his forties, and Therese was still in her twenties. It was revealed later that Joe had been in prison, but Therese had only found out about his past after the wedding. I had heard from my parents that he was abusive toward my sister; I do not know how far the abuse went.

Though the specific motive for Therese's death is unclear, Therese was clearly distraught and, after Tom's suicide, she and others in our family had struggled with depression and suicidal thoughts.

TURNING AWAY HELP, COMPOUNDING MY PAIN

While this moment was obviously tragic for me, I managed to get through the Thanksgiving weekend and return to St. Francis the following Monday. Counseling was offered but not required. I turned down the offer and just pushed forward. Of course, I had managed to bottle up my pain. In fact, before the funeral of my sister and brother-in-law, I was already back in school. I hardly talked about her death with my friends at the seminary.

On the Monday following Thanksgiving, while walking to philosophy class, a fellow University of San Diego student reported to me how angry he was. He said his friend had been jogging in our canyon that weekend when he came upon a woman who had hanged herself. He said that his friend had suffered great trauma after seeing the sight and that he was "pissed" at the woman for making his friend suffer.

That was my sister he was talking about. Of course, I didn't have the courage to tell him. All I know is that I found myself staring at a statue of our Blessed Mother resting on top of the Immaculata church there on campus. I remember feeling a sense of peace as I let him express his feelings. It was as if Mary was saying, "Even in your pain, just be there for him." It was one of the most surreal yet profound moments in my life.

After a few months, I was in the running for the seminary's senior-class president. When I lost the election, I was told by a few seminarians that their decision not to elect me was based on my siblings' suicides. Needless to say, I was furious. I was mad at them; I was mad at the newly elected president; I was mad at Tom, Therese, and Joe; and I was mad at God. I stormed out of the seminary and to the end of a field at the University of San Diego where I could be by myself. There, I tore into God. I let loose! I asked God to just end my life then and there.

After a good cry, I went back to the seminary and went to bed. I wasn't sure what I was going to do the next day. I was still mad, embarrassed, and ashamed to be a victim of sibling suicide. I hated the fact that I was labeled as different. It hurt.

Somehow, the next morning, I managed to thank God for taking my anger. I justified my outburst by saying that God was big enough to take it, and he would probably rather have me yell at him than curse my friends. Once again, I pushed on.

Even after the suicides of Therese and Joe I went without counseling. The rector of St. Francis Seminary suggested some therapy, but I passed on the offer. He never pursued it again.

I was later accepted to St. Patrick's Seminary in Menlo Park, California, for theological studies. Again I went through the necessary battery of tests for entrance, but the suicidal trend in my family did not come up as an issue. I continued on until my senior year, when one faculty member saw my psychological report and urged the faculty to confront me on my family's history. After their numerous requests for me to see their counselor, the faculty finally insisted on a psychological review. I was ready for ordination to the diaconate and they wanted assurance that I would be ready to accept the challenges of ministry in the Church. Seeing no alternative, I begrudgingly went for counseling and after six sessions I was given the green light to continue toward ordination. I was ordained to the diaconate and then to the priesthood on July 1, 1989, for the Diocese of San Diego.

FINDING HELP FOR MY WOUNDS

Only after having some normal up-and-down ministerial experiences as a young priest did I begin to see the value of seeking counseling on my own. As a thirteen-year-old boy, my maturation was stunted, and as a young priest it was finally dawning on me that I had to deal with this identity crisis.

I discovered in just a few sessions that the daily routine of priesthood was not fitting nicely with the savior image that I had hoped for. Admittedly, many young priests struggle with a savior complex and most are able to quickly realize that there is only one true Savior of the world. Unfortunately for me, it took a little longer. I think this was due in large part to posttraumatic stress I experienced after my brother's suicide.

I requested a leave of absence from ministry from my bishop. Moved by the grace of God, I began to review my life. This meant going back to my beginnings.

Returning to my baptism, where I was born again as a beloved child of Christ, I re-presented myself as his Father's son. For the first time as a priest, I took seriously my identity as a Christian in the fullest sense of the word. I was suddenly more at peace with myself than I had ever been. Reclaiming my share in the divinity of Christ, who humbled himself to share in my broken humanity, I was ready to hear the words of my dad, "Be yourself!" During the leave of absence, I decided to see a counselor on a regular basis. I also found a spiritual director and reconnected with some of my old priesthood friends. To this day, I maintain all three avenues of support. This support system allows me to stay focused on my identity as a Christian. To know who I am means to know where I am going.

After returning to ministry, I threw myself into the life of my parish community with a fervent love for the Lord and his Church. My intent was to remain in parish ministry for the rest of my priestly life. God had other plans. Although my journey as bishop today can be heavily administrative, and although I am not embedded in the joys of parish life, I am more joyful than ever. I abide in his love who has loved me first. Sharing in the divinity of the one who humbled himself to share in my humanity is joy enough for me. This is both my identity and my journey. In order to help me abide in my Christian identity and mission, I pray. I pray a lot. I stay connected with our Blessed Mother, I celebrate the sacraments, and I pursue the virtuous life with a special focus on faith, hope, and love.

FINDING PEACE IN CHRIST

I am back living in an apartment at St. Francis Seminary on the University of San Diego campus. Each day, I walk on the campus praying the Rosary. Halfway through, I stop at the field where I cried and cursed at God on that night in the seminary. The field is now replaced by the Joan B. Kroc Institute for Peace and Justice building. There, I now thank God for peace. I offer a thanksgiving of peace, not because I'm a bishop or even a priest. I thank God for gracing me with the profound gift of being his son. I am his beloved. So too are my brother Tom, my sister Therese, and her husband, Joe. As I have found peace, may they rest in peace.

This is my story. My parents and my siblings each have their own stories as they each are survivors of suicide loss. If you are a survivor of one who died by suicide, you will have your own story. Tell your story. It will only bring growth. But if your story does not begin and end with being yourself, with the unique Christian self that God has made you to be, your journey will be difficult and your story will be incomplete. Christ never wanted our journeys to be difficult. In him, even with tragedies and daily crosses, we can find joy. Only in Christ will we have complete joy.

KEY POINTS

- Grief does not go away, no matter how much we try to hide it.
- Grief affects everyone differently.
- We need to tell our own stories.
- We need to accept help from many places—counseling, spiritual direction, and the support of family and friends.

ASK YOURSELF

1. Have mental illness and suicide affected my family? In what ways?
2. What did my family teach me about dealing with grief? What has been helpful? What has not been helpful?
3. What supports do I have in my life—psychological, spiritual, personal, and familial? What can I do to strengthen these supports?
4. Who needs to hear my story? When and how will I tell my story?

5. How can I help people with whom I minister tell their stories of distress due to psychological disorder, mental illness, and suicide?

2.

A Grief Revealed and Redeemed

THE DEATH OF MY SISTER, MARY ANNE POPE

Msgr. Charles Pope
Archdiocese of Washington, DC

My sister, Mary Anne Pope, was born on April 2, 1960, the first child of Charles and Nancy Pope. Mary Anne was tragically afflicted with mental illness from her earliest days. Because she did not speak a word until she was well past two, and even then only at home, my parents knew something was wrong. Discretion and brevity limit what I intend to share here, but even as little children, my brother George and I knew something was very wrong with our sister. Her erratic behavior made her shift from moments of fearful shyness to rather exotic actions that were either violent or just strange. Indeed, Mary Anne was deeply troubled.

MENTAL ILLNESS AFFECTS THE WHOLE FAMILY

My sister, Mary Anne, had a pathological shyness that led her to shut down in the presence of others outside the home. The counselor at her elementary school spoke of Mary Anne as "disturbed" and insisted on psychiatric care for her by the time she was six. I remember when I was very young my mother bringing Mary Anne to her counselor. She explained that Mary Anne was "shy" and that her friend was helping her feel better.

13

At one point in early 1970, aware that Mary Anne felt isolated in the house with two brothers and desperately wanted a sister, my parents even went so far as to seek to adopt a baby girl. They filed paperwork and came very close, but the plan ultimately fell through and we never had a baby sister. By age eleven Mary Anne was running away from home. During this period and throughout her lifetime my parents made many sacrifices for Mary Anne, both financial and personal, to ensure her care.

When Mary Anne was thirteen, my parents found such deeply disturbing plans in her diary that mental health professionals advised and insisted that she had to be hospitalized. She spent the remainder of her life in fifteen different mental hospitals and six different group homes. Her diagnosis was paranoid schizophrenia.

She was often able to visit with us and even stay over on weekend passes. She had stretches during which she was stable, but soon the voices and dreams that afflicted her would return. Her psychotic episodes often led to running away, outbursts of violence, vandalism, shop lifting, setting fires, and cutting her wrists and other attempts at suicide.

Through all these years, my parents, in their grief and love, fought very hard for her, and they insisted she get the care she needed, despite insurance and governmental systems that increasingly consigned the mentally ill to life on the streets. This battle often led my parents to various courts and generated much correspondence with insurance companies, state mental health officials, and private hospitals where my sister was confined.

On one critical occasion my mother was summoned to a mental institution where my sister was residing. Mary Anne was standing on the roof of the five-story building, planning to jump. Police and fire officials were trying to call her off the edge. In the midst of this, my mother sensed the Lord speaking to her these words: "Mary Anne is more my daughter than yours. Whatever happens today, I want you to know that I love her and that she is in my care."

UNDERSTANDING AT THE LAST

Mary Anne died in a fire in the winter of 1991 at the age of thirty-one. At the time, I was thirty years old and an associate pastor at my first parish assignment. The fire investigators concluded that the fire was no accident and declared her death a suicide. Indeed, Mary Anne had set fires before when the voices told her to.

A great sadness in my life is that it took Mary Anne's death for me to recognize her dignity and see her true suffering. I had often avoided talking to her. She often tried to speak of her unusual dreams and her need for attention, but I made excuses and privately complained to my parents of her unwanted requests to talk.

But four days after her death I looked right into the face of her pain. The funeral directors explained that they had made her presentable enough for the immediate family to briefly view her body. They explained, however, that her features were delicate since the fire had singed her upper body. Thus they could not work much on her appearance or adjust the expression on her face. We gathered, for a last look, and it was then that I saw it. She had clearly died weeping. Yes, I could see the pain on her face as her body lay in the casket and I wept deeply when I saw her. All of us did. Poor Mary Anne; poor, poor Mary Anne. It was a grief revealed. A very deep grief. Her life must have been riddled with grief, with suffering and grieving for a life she would never have.

How could I have missed my sister's grief for all those years? Was it my fear of her? Was it my annoyance? Perhaps it was my frustration at not being able to do anything to make my sister better. But such grief I had missed.

She had often talked of her dream to get well, marry, and be happy. I thought it was a crazy dream. But more likely it was her crying out, an expression of her grief and her pain at her tormented dreams and the voices that filled her mind with irrational fears. She just wanted to be well, normal, and happy. I missed all this; I missed her pain. But that day, looking one last time at her, I saw it, fixed there in her final expression. "Mary Anne," I thought, "how little I really knew you or understood your pain. I am so sorry I missed it. I am sorry I did not understand. I am so sorry it took your death for me to know your grief and sorrow. May it never again be so, dear Mary Anne, that I miss the dignity of those close to me who suffer."

Not long after her funeral, perhaps a day or two, I was celebrating a daily Mass and it was for her repose. Just after Communion, as I was purifying the vessels, I heard my sister's voice. It was not some internal conviction—it was a voice, her voice. She said, "I'm okay now, Charlie." To be clear, I am not one who hears voices or sees things. Yet so certain was I that I had heard a real voice, I asked the congregants, "Did you hear that?" I received only blank stares and a few looks that said no.

But I knew what I had heard. It was a consolation I did not think I deserved. She could never have said "I'm okay now" in this world. It rang true, and it sounded like her manner of speaking. Yes, I was sure it was her. Thank you, Lord, for that undeserved grace, which continues to bless my life!

THE RIPPLING EFFECTS OF DEATH BY SUICIDE

Suicide, of course, is a crushing blow for family members who experience such loss. This is so even in the cases of clear mental illness, as with my sister. My mother carried a special burden that I suppose only a mother knows. In the weeks and months that followed Mary Anne's death, she often wept and said simply, "My daughter, my beautiful daughter, Mary Anne."

Sadly, my mother's grief grew steadily worse, causing her struggle with alcohol to worsen. She had been something of a drinker all her life, but it was mostly maintenance and self-medication. Through her forties and early fifties she had been a popular and successful schoolteacher at the local Catholic school. But her grief caused her to retire the year after my sister's death. At this point my mother's alcoholism went fully active and she became increasingly incapacitated: car accidents, medical issues, treatment centers, attempt after attempt to get free—all the tragic stuff of alcoholism.

In all of this I strove not to forget the lesson my sister had taught me. While at times I was angry at my mother for her drinking, I did not want it to take her death for me to see and honor her grief, pain, and dignity. I went steadily to Al-Anon meetings to stay sane myself, and I honored my mother's many struggles to get free. I saw that her grief was something to be respected and not dismissed.

The life of my mother, Nancy Pope, ended tragically and suddenly on a cold February day in 2005. My father had looked away for only a brief moment, going into the kitchen to make a sandwich, and Mom wandered out into the cold and into the face of an impending snowstorm. Incapacitated by alcohol and disoriented, she died that night of hypothermia. We found her body only after three days of searching, when the snow melted a bit. She had died almost a mile away, near the edge of the woods. In her death it was a grief revealed: it was *her* grief—her deep, deep grief, a sorrow that stretched back some fifteen years to my sister's death.

My father never quite forgave himself for letting Mom slip away. The open front door was a first sign of trouble—a troubled night that grew increasingly awful as our frantic searching on a dark, frigid, and snowy night brought the steady and awful awareness that she was gone. Yes, those memories haunted my father.

In the months that followed, he often wondered how he could go on when half of him was gone. He often spoke of wanting to be with his Nancy, and he was gone within two years. His congestive heart failure worsened in those two years, and my dad, Charles Pope, died in 2007, literally and figuratively of a broken heart. It was a grief revealed.

After my father's death in 2007, and except for essential papers related to his estate, I simply boxed up most of his papers and stored them in the attic of my rectory for future attention. A few years later I was sorting through those boxes. Among his effects were many papers, both his and my mother's. In particular, I was struck by the poignant file that was simply labeled "Mary Anne." My father wrote this on the frontispiece of her file:

> Mary Anne Pope was our first child.
> She led a tortured existence during a short life
> and fought hard against great odds.
> We remember her for her courage.

And as I read the historical data and my own parents' touching recollections of Mary Anne within the file, I could not help but be moved, too, by their own pain. Such a heavy grief punctuates each page. I give them great credit for the fact that they insulated the rest of us, their three sons, from the most dreadful details of Mary Anne's struggle. They kept their pain largely to themselves and stayed available to us. It is true that there were episodes we had to know about, but as a young boy and teenager I saw in my parents only strength and stability when it came to this matter.

Something of their pain is evident in those short lines of my father on the cover of her file. It was their grief revealed.

JESUS UNDERSTANDS SUICIDE: MARY ANNE CAN SEE THE GLORY OF GOD

An old spiritual says, "Nobody knows the trouble I've seen. Nobody knows but Jesus." And it is a mighty good thing that he *does* know. Sometimes the grief is too heavy even to share, even to put into words. But Jesus knows all about our troubles. As I have said, I deeply regret that I did not understand my sister's grief or pain until she died. My parents too often carried their pain quietly, and I cannot say I ever really knew their pain until I saw the file labeled simply "Mary Anne." But I am glad of this much: Jesus knew.

It is true, my sister Mary Anne died in a suicidal fire. But she was just too mentally ill and tormented by voices to be fully responsible for it. All that matters to me is that Jesus knew. She often called on him, and one fiery night when the pain was too great, I am convinced in faith that he called her home as if through fire (see 1 Corinthians 3:15).

Something tells me that I will have to get an appointment to see Mary Anne in heaven, since she will be close to the throne of God. Jesus says, "And the last will be first" (Mt 19:30). Mother Mary says that God lifts up the lowly (Lk 1:52).

Yes, those who have suffered much but with faith will be exulted in heaven and be closest to God. My parents, too, surely saw their glory increased through their sufferings (see 2 Corinthians 4:10–15).

There is a beautiful line in the book of Revelation that refers to those who have died in the Lord: "He will wipe every tear from their eyes, and there shall be no more death or mourning, wailing or pain, [for] the old order has passed away. The one who sat on the throne said, 'Behold, I make all things new'"(Rv 21:4–5).

For my brave parents and courageous sister, who all died in the Lord but who died with grief, I pray that this text has already been fulfilled and that they now enjoy everything that is new, their tears are wiped away, and their grief has been redeemed.

Requiescant in pace.

KEY POINTS

- Mental illness is a family issue.
- The pain and suffering caused by mental illness is real and can be unrelenting.
- Christ loves and understands people who suffered from mental illness and died by suicide.
- The death of child, by suicide or in any other way, is something a parent never gets over. It is a grief a parent will always live with.
- Give your grief to Christ and you will know peace.

ASK YOURSELF

1. How does my own fear, ignorance, and lack of understanding about mental illness affect my ability to support people who live with mental illness and psychological pain?
2. How do I see Christ in those who live with serious mental illness, such as schizophrenia?
3. What I can do to ensure that I engage the deep grief that others are experiencing with respect, acceptance, and even embrace?
4. How can I support the belief that someone who has died by suicide can be okay, resting in the compassionate presence of our loving God?

3.

The Suicide Death of My Daughter, Katie

Deacon Ed Shoener
Diocese of Scranton

We know that all things work for good for those who love God.

—Romans 8:28

I am told everyone reacts differently when the knock comes at your door and you find out your child is dead. It was a knock that my wife, Ruth, and I hoped would never come—but one that for more than eleven years we had worried would come.

It was a few minutes before midnight on a warm Wednesday night in August. The doorbell suddenly started ringing rapidly and there was loud knocking on our front door. I was upstairs in our bedroom with Ruth, and we were just getting to sleep. I said to Ruth, "This can't be good."

Ruth got to the door first and opened it. She said nothing, but she looked at me startled. I got to the door to see two police officers and immediately knew why they were there. Not a word was spoken until I asked, "It's Katie, isn't it?"

The officers came in and we walked to the kitchen in quiet, in shock, but strangely composed. We all sat at the kitchen table and I answered their questions. I was given the phone number of the officer in Ohio who found Katie and who was conducting the investigation. Katie lived near Columbus; we lived then and still do in Scranton, Pennsylvania. I called the officer immediately.

The officer in Ohio told me Katie died from a gunshot to her head. He had to ask difficult questions for the investigation. I assured him it was suicide—not a murder. I explained that Katie had lived with bipolar disorder for more than eleven years. She had attempted suicide before and struggled with intense suicidal thoughts. I asked him when we could bring her body home. The detective explained that the county coroner needed to conclude the investigation before we could do that.

I begged him to please finish the investigation quickly—that we wanted to bring our little girl home. It was at this point that I began to feel pain through the shock. It came slowly at first. Some tears as I talked to the officer. Ruth and I looked at each other, and we were just so, so sad. But we kept ourselves under control, showed the officers out, and thanked them for being so kind. We said we knew that it was not easy for them to give parents this news. Then they quietly left our house.

More pain than I had ever felt hit me then, and hit hard. Ruth put her head down on the table. She weakened under the pain. She just cried and cried and cried inconsolably.

I had never known what it is to wail. It goes beyond tears. It is visceral. It is primordial. It comes from a place most of us never know exists within us. It is tears and screaming and physical pain. I went out on our deck and pounded our wooden table. I screamed and sobbed. Our son Bill built the table and made it strong and sturdy. I don't know how long I pounded on it. I pounded until I was exhausted.

At some point Ruth and I fell into each other's arms. Two became one. We needed each other. We were one stream of tears, like blood flowing from a wound. There is nothing sentimental about love at this moment. It is raw. It is horrible. Yet, in the face of death, it is life-giving. It is strong, and it goes beyond all understanding. No words are spoken. Words are not possible or needed. Love is needed.

KATIE'S MENTAL ILLNESS

Eventually Ruth and I started to talk. We did not know what else could have been done. Katie had done everything she was told to do by her doctors. She took all her medicines. She did not use drugs and was not addicted to anything. Ruth talked to Katie every day—every single day. Katie's family loved her. She loved all of us and she had many friends. She had recently graduated with her MBA from the Fisher College of Business at Ohio State University and wanted to work in human resource management because she loved helping people succeed.

We knew that Katie did not want to die by suicide. She wanted to live. She had attempted suicide before, and she was afraid of it. She had checked into a hospital several times when the suicidal thoughts were intense. She knew that suicide makes no sense. But mental illness is not rational. This illness told her that she was terrible, a burden, no one liked or loved her, and that she was a useless mistake. She was in deep and irrational pain.

Mental illness is as evil and unrelenting as cancer, heart disease, or any other malady. For many people it can be treated and managed. Katie was treated by therapists and psychiatrists, and she took medicines for her type 1 bipolar disorder. Like chemotherapy for cancer, which can help people live longer than they would have without the chemotherapy, the medicines kept Katie alive for many years. But in her last year the medicines slowly stopped working. Her mental illness overwhelmed her and became lethal.

GOD'S GRACE AND KATIE'S OBITUARY

Ruth and I finally went to bed the night our daughter died, but sleep was impossible. Full-on dad instincts kicked in for me. I felt a need to do what I could for my little girl. I got up and called the funeral director in the middle of the night. We talked about getting her home, about making funeral arrangements, about all the things you never want to do for your child. But at this moment you do them—and you want to do them well. Katie still needed to be taken care of.

I decided I needed to write Katie's obituary. Ruth asked me what I was doing at the computer. It was the middle of the night and only a couple of hours since the police knocked on our door. How, she wondered, could I possibly be able to write anything? But I wanted our friends, neighbors, and parishioners to know what happened so that there would not be any gossip or hushed talk. I wanted them to know that Katie was a good girl who had a terrible illness. So, with the grace of God, I wrote Katie's obituary that night.

> Kathleen "Katie" Marie Shoener, 29, fought bipolar disorder since 2005, but she finally lost the battle to suicide on Wednesday in Lewis Center, Ohio.
>
> So often, people who have a mental illness are known as their illness. People say that "she is bipolar" or "he is schizophrenic." Over the coming days as you talk to people about this, please do not use that phrase. People who have cancer are not cancer, those with diabetes are not diabetes. Katie was not bipolar—she had an illness called bipolar disorder. Katie herself was a beautiful child of God. The way we talk about people and their illnesses affects the people themselves and how we treat the illness. In the case of mental illness, there is so much fear, ignorance, and hurtful attitudes that the people who suffer from mental illness needlessly suffer further.

Our society does not provide the resources that are needed to adequately understand and treat mental illness. In Katie's case, she had the best medical care available, she always took the cocktail of medicines that she was prescribed, and she did her best to be healthy and manage this illness. And yet, that was not enough. Someday a cure will be found, but until then, we need to support and be compassionate to those with mental illness, every bit as much as we support those who suffer from cancer, heart disease, diabetes, or any other illness.

Please know that Katie was a sweet, wonderful person who loved life, the people around her—and Jesus Christ.

Early that morning we made the calls you never want to make to your children. We called Katie's three brothers—Rob, Bill, and Eddie—to tell them that their sister died by suicide. It was hard to hear the anguish, deep sorrow, and weeping from them.

I sent out an email to my colleagues at my business with the obituary and asked for their patience while I took time for Katie's funeral. I also sent an email with the obituary to the staff at St. Peters Cathedral in Scranton, where I am a permanent deacon. And then I went to the 8:00 a.m. Mass at the cathedral—the daily Mass I regularly attend.

CLINGING TO CHRIST, BROKEN FOR US

I was drawn to the Eucharist that morning with the strongest pull I had ever felt to attend a Mass. I entered the sacristy and saw Fr. Jeff Walsh and others talking about the news of Katie's death. They were surprised to see me. But where else would I go to find solace?

I asked to preach and explained to the small congregation why I needed to be at the Mass that morning. I read Katie's obituary—slowly, so that I would not sob and be incoherent—because it was important that they heard the message clearly.

Like the love between Ruth and me when we had received the news just a few hours earlier, there is nothing remote and sentimental about the love that Christ offers at Mass. His love, then as always, was direct, and I felt it. His Passion and Death were united to Katie's death and to my grief during that Mass. He held me up. He was with me. Christ went into my darkness, like walking into a tomb, to be with me. Katie was broken, I was broken, and Christ's body was also broken for us at the altar, as it is at every Mass. Christ was suffering with my family and me. His presence in the Eucharist was never more real to me.

At the end of Mass, I went down the aisle to greet the small group of people who attend the morning Mass. I needed to be surrounded by this small Christian community that I worship with each day. Again, it was not remote and sentimental; it was instead direct and real. All pretenses fell away.

In a community united in Christ, there is grief and sorrow, yet there is also strength and love; we lift one another up. Even if it was only a simple "I am so sorry," I could see in my community members' eyes the love of Christ as they said it. I knew once again Christ was broken for me by their compassion and loving presence.

I was scheduled to see my spiritual director, Fr. Jim Redington, for our monthly meeting that morning right after Mass. I kept the appointment. I walked the few blocks from the cathedral to the Jesuit residence at the University of Scranton, where my spiritual director lives. I told him about Katie. He knew how it felt to lose someone you love to suicide, telling me his brother died this way.

I am a spiritual director myself, and one of the fundamental beliefs about spiritual direction is that in every session there are three people—the directee, the director, and the Holy Spirit. Usually the directee does most of the talking, the director asks questions and offers guidance, and both listen in their hearts for the Holy Spirit. At our session that morning, we went into the small chapel of Fr. Jim's residence and simply sat in adoration of the Eucharist. I could not talk, and he knew there was nothing he could say that would help right then. Only the Holy Spirit spoke that morning. We were enveloped in Love.

I was given the gift of God's peace on the most horrible morning of my life: at Mass, with the support of my faith community, and while in eucharistic adoration with a holy priest who understood my pain. The peace of the Lord was with my spirit.

THE VIRAL OBITUARY

The rest of that day was filled with calls and visits from family and friends, all deeply appreciated. That afternoon I went to meet with our funeral director to work out the details of the funeral. Ruth stayed at home to be with our family. I selected a white casket for Katie. White is the color of hope—hope in the Resurrection.

Among the many other things that had to be done, we also put the details of the funeral into Katie's obituary and sent it to the local newspaper for publication in both the hard copy of the newspaper and the online version. It appeared the next day.

I had hoped the obituary would encourage an open and honest conversation about mental illness and Katie's suicide in our small town of Scranton, but what actually happened was totally unexpected. The response to Katie's obituary was incredible. It went viral in social media. It was picked up by newspapers through-out the United States and around the world. There was television and radio cov-erage. Katie's obituary was seen by millions of people, as headlines appeared in places near and far.

> She "Loved Life": A Grieving Father Wrote Openly about Suicide and Mental Illness in Daughter's Obituary
>
> *Washington Post*[1]

> Katie Committed Suicide in a Bipolar Crisis and Her Father Wrote in the Obituary a Message to Humanity
>
> *Visão*, Lisbon, Portugal[2]

> Parents Use Daughter's Obituary to Discuss the Stigmas around Mental Health
>
> *Yahoo News*[3]

> Grieving Father's Commonsense Message about Mental Illness Is a Wake-Up Call
>
> *Dallas Morning News*[4]

> She Loved Life—a Father in Mourning Writes of the Suicide of Daughter with a Mental Illness
>
> *Urban Post*, Livorno, Italy[5]

> On the Deacon's Daughter Who Committed Suicide: "God Will Use This Death to Help Others Come Out of the Shadows"
>
> *The Deacon's Bench*[6]

> This Father Used His Daughter's Obituary to Make an Important Point about the Way We Treat People with Mental Health Issues
>
> *The Independent*, United Kingdom[7]

I am convinced, beyond any shadow of doubt, that God used Katie's obituary to deliver his message of love. God did not create Katie to have a mental illness and die by suicide; he created her to be the beautiful and vibrant person that we all knew and loved. Yet we live in a broken world where there is sin, illness, and death. All this evil will be completely defeated in eternal life, but evil is also overcome every day in this life as God pours out his love on us in the small things of life, such as Katie's obituary, as signs of what is to come in eternal life. God overcame Katie's tragic death by using her obituary to help people understand that he is with them in their struggle with mental illness and he has mercy on those who die by suicide.

Some people took the time to write touching notes about what Katie's obituary meant to them on her obituary page at Legacy.com;[8] there were thousands of comments on Facebook pages, in various blogs, and in the comment sections of online newspapers. Here are just a few examples:

I have lost many family and friends to suicide caused by a mental illness and frankly, no one wants to talk about it. It's shameful, you're frowned upon, and you are labeled as being crazy. Well this is a very common illness that needs to be addressed and this obituary will hopefully sway people to open up and talk about it before we lose more lives to this battle. I pray that as unfortunate as this is that even now God is using this for a good divine purpose, to educate others to be compassionate, to avoid being quick to judge because it can happen to you or anyone. May God shower you all with his comfort and strength knowing Kathleen's not suffering anymore and that the way she left this earth is not in vain; there is a divine purpose and it started with Kathleen's obituary.

Anonymous

As someone who has struggled with depression, I have often found it difficult to speak to people about my illness due to the stigma and ignorance that surrounds it. Thank you for what you have written, thank you for helping to dispel the negativity surrounding mental illness, thank you for helping us. May the Lord bless you and keep you.

Baton Rouge, Louisiana

We need more people discussing the realities of struggling with a mental illness and, just as you say, that it can be as difficult, painful, and sometimes terminal as any other serious illness. I am bipolar and it's a constant battle. People have a difficult time understanding how I struggle, and the horrible pain of depressive episodes or cycling so much that my thinking is only realistic when I have some stability, on meds and the challenge to even getting stable enough to mimic a decent life at least, for a while. We need to break through the stigma. Most people are afraid of the term. They usually conjure images of people being psychotic, running through the streets, naked. They don't realize the many, different facets of BP. I hope the discussion continues.

San Jose, California

I am twenty-two years old and have bipolar disorder. I was diagnosed last year but have struggled since I was fourteen. I wish I had known Katie, because our stories are incredibly similar. I love God with all my heart, as Katie did. I struggle every day and the stigma behind bipolar holds me back from getting all the support I need. Katie's life brought so much joy and learning to others and her passing has brought healing and hope to many. I think that's the best kind of life well lived, even though her pain was greater than she could bear.

Anonymous

Your touching story about Katie's life and her struggles with bipolar disease has led me to reach out for help for the first time (I am fifty-three). Katie's story has greatly impacted my life and the lives of many others that suffer from bipolar disease.

Cheboygan, Michigan

I read Kathleen's story and it brought me back to when I was a teen. I, too, suffered in silence my whole life. We had so much in common. I did the same thing in high school with the pills and slashing, being on meds for years. I've seen therapists, yet nothing has helped with my disorder. I've been suicidal many times and I'm afraid that day will happen. I hope there's a cure before I give up the fight. I'm only forty-eight. So sorry for your loss. I know exactly how she felt.

Halifax, Nova Scotia

My prayers to you and your family, may God comfort you. You have lived through my greatest fear. My twenty-one-year-old daughter has been fighting bi-polar since she was twelve. We have seen her thru suicide attempts, crippling depression, self-harm, and hospitalizations, interspersed with periods of stability, joy, and shining talent. My daughter is stable for now, but there is always the fear. I have shared your post with my friends and family, as you have so eloquently expressed what this is like. Thank you for sharing, and my deepest sympathies to you all.

Maryland

I lost my husband on June 17, 2016, to suicide. He also suffered from bipolar disorder. I shared this on my Facebook page because I think so many people need to read this, and perhaps if they do and truly understand what you've laid out, in some small way it might begin to chip away at the stigma of mental illness. I have never understood why people treat those with mental illness differently than people with physical illness. Thank you for your insight. My prayers and thoughts go out to you and your family.

Anchorage, Alaska

As someone who has almost taken my life many times, my heart goes out to the family of this beautiful, talented young woman. Our system is broken, and it hurts that no matter how hard Kathleen tried, she still struggled. Those medications are not easy to take or tolerate, and she so clearly wanted to get better if she was so diligent about them. We as a society need to understand and do better. May her family find light in God and in continuing to raise awareness for mental health care in Kathleen's name during this dark time.

Boonton, New Jersey

CHANGED FOREVER

As consoling as all the notes and comments were, Ruth and I will, of course, always dearly miss Katie. Everyone whom I have spoken with who has buried a child has said there will always be a hole in our hearts. The shock has subsided, and we have gotten back to working and enjoying life, but we are forever changed.

The death of a child, especially by suicide, puts a tremendous strain and burden on a marriage. Depression, loneliness, and perhaps anger move in. All too often it leads to divorce. Ruth and I are fortunate that our marriage has endured, but our marriage has changed. Grief is now a part of our marriage. Ruth and I grieve differently, but we can grieve together. We were bound together in a thousand ways, but now we are also bound together in Katie's death. In a mysterious way, the grace of the Holy Spirit that is part of the Sacrament of Marriage has carried us in our grief.

At times our grief felt almost unbearable. Although its intensity has diminished with time, it has not gone away. We still think about Katie and her death every day. Everyone I have spoken to who has lost a child says the same. The grief that comes with losing a child is different from what comes with other losses. It is intense, and it is long lasting; perhaps it is forever. We need to pray for those who are living with the death of a child and we need to pray for marriages that face this grief.

FINDING KATIE

From time to time I pray at Katie's grave to grieve. There is a simple stone with a cross and her favorite saying engraved on it: "Be Awesome." But I know I will not find Katie at her grave. I know Katie is with the Risen Christ.

As the angels said on the morning of the Resurrection, "Why do you seek the living one among the dead? He is not here, but he has been raised" (Lk 24:5–6). Christ is not dead but lives eternally. A fundamental truth of our faith is that Christ is in us and in everyone we encounter. Therefore I will find Christ among the living, and where I find Christ is also where I will find Katie because Katie is with the Risen Christ. Both are among the living.[9]

We can find our loved ones in the things that they loved and in the things they struggled with, just as we can find Christ in our own loves and struggles. Katie loved to be around people, yet she struggled with mental illness and died by suicide. So, I find Katie not by grieving alone but by being around people and serving those who struggle with mental illness. In a special way, I see Christ in people who grieve a loved one who died by suicide.

Death is not the final word; even the tragedy of death by suicide is not the final word. The Word of God overcomes death and transforms it to new life. We can participate in this new life by seeing in the death of our loved ones an inspiration to build up the kingdom of God. We overcome the death of a loved one by taking what they loved and bringing that love to the world. We can take the suffering of our lives and transform it into loving service to others who suffer with what they suffered.

KEY POINTS

- Mental illness is an illness, not a character flaw or a moral failing.
- We must see people who live with mental illness as beautiful creations of God and not define them by the illness.
- Because of stigma and how we treat mental illness, the people who suffer from mental illness needlessly suffer further.
- The medical care for mental illness is not adequate and needs to be significantly improved.
- The death of a child, especially by suicide, puts great strains on a family and on marriages.
- God can transform even the evil of suicide and turn it to help others.

ASK YOURSELF

1. What have been my misconceptions about people who live with mental illness?
2. What can I do to help stop stigmatizing people who live with mental illness?
3. What can I do to advocate for better mental health care?
4. How can I honor the memory of the people I know who have died by suicide?

4.

Praying after a Suicide Loss

Leticia Adams
Catholic Writer and Speaker
Austin, Texas

My son Anthony died from suicide in 2017. He was twenty-two years old and had an entire life ahead of him. My idea of God, Catholicism, and everything associated with it was changed that day. I cursed God, I cried to God, I questioned God. But now I know that God walked beside me the whole time and that he loves Anthony more than I did then or do now. Let me tell you my story—the story of a mom whose son died by suicide and how through the sacraments I was able to pray again and find consolation and hope.

DETERMINED TO BE A "GOOD" CATHOLIC

I converted to Catholicism in 2010 after a life of "looking for love in all the wrong places," as the song goes. That was a reaction to childhood trauma, which included being sexually abused. I came to a parish with a brand-new priest, a great pastor, and a RCIA director who not only understood the teachings of the Catholic Church but also knew Jesus. At this parish I found the one place where all my questions were answered, and I did not freak people out.

I encountered God on my second night of RCIA in the parking lot of the parish as I sat in my car thinking about the words of our director, Noe Rocha, when he looked at me and said, "God loves you more than you think he does. No matter how far you have gone, he loves you and wants you back." I could not

29

know then that in seven years Noe would be standing in the sanctuary of our parish reading the second reading at my son's funeral following his suicide.

Because I came into the Catholic Church after a crazy life of drinking too much, sleeping around, and being an irresponsible parent, when I was initiated into the Church and then married in the Church, I figured life would be smooth sailing. I went to daily Mass and monthly Confession. I was involved in a variety of ministries in my parish. I helped Noe with RCIA and anything else he had going on. I was determined to be a "good" Catholic. This included making sure my children were baptized and that we all went to Mass every Sunday.

My oldest son, Anthony, resisted, especially when he got into his teenage years and into girls. We had some huge arguments. Eventually Anthony was old enough to decide for himself, and he decided to stop going to Mass. He also told me he was no longer a Catholic and instead he was an atheist.

LIFE HAPPENS

Anthony saved my life when I got pregnant with him in 1993, when I was sixteen years old. He gave me something to live for. He loved me when I didn't love myself, and he was my best friend. It was an honor to be his mother and watch him grow into a wonderful father. A talented artist since he could hold a pencil, Anthony also loved to skate, work out, rent movies, bury his younger brother in the backyard, play video games, and shave his eyebrows to annoy his mother. He was always willing to help anyone he could, however he could. He was respectful, kind, and responsible.

After Anthony broke with Catholicism, the next few years brought some extreme changes, both good and bad. A good swing brought the births of Anthony's two beautiful daughters. But the deaths of a number of close family members took a toll on all of us. For Anthony, the death of my uncle in 2016, when Anthony was twenty-one years old, was particularly difficult because Anthony was very close to my uncle.

In the months following my uncle's death, Anthony had a mental breakdown of some kind. Once, we got him to the doctor in the middle of what we thought was a psychotic episode, which the doctor confirmed, but Anthony refused treatment. When he got home with his friends, he told them that the doctor had said there was nothing wrong with him. This was not true, of course.

For the next ten months I prayed in every way I could think of for Anthony. He was not well. He was having delusions, and he was paranoid that people were going to hurt his children. He was a lot to deal with. Even though he had moved out of our house and was living with his fiancée and children in their own apartment, his illness took a toll on all of us as a family.

Anthony had always been someone who could help me with his younger siblings, either by managing behavioral issues or by giving them rides to places they needed to be. Suddenly he was no longer reliable, and his siblings felt as though he was no longer available to them as their big brother. That was extremely difficult for them to understand. Anthony was waking me up at all hours of the night with phone calls because he was worried someone was trying to get into his apartment (all delusions and paranoia). He was upsetting his siblings with his angry outbursts, which was not like him at all. His behavior was chaotic and unpredictable. All these things pointed to him having some mental illness issues, but he would not agree to see a doctor, so there was never a diagnosis. Yet he was also scared by his behavior, and in moments of clarity he would say that he was sorry for being difficult.

Ten months after my uncle died, his wife died and Anthony took the news very hard. I made a point to check in with him a lot after this. It was also when I began to fear him hurting himself. I have never prayed as much as I prayed for Anthony during those next months. I was terrified of something, but I had no idea what that something was going to be. I just knew the possibility was that it would be very bad.

ANTHONY'S GONE

I went to a parish to venerate the relics of St. Anthony of Padua, whom my son was named after. I prayed for God to help my son find his way back to the Church and for Anthony's salvation. I took the prayer card I got and gave it to Anthony. But he was gone just days later. On March 8, 2017, my husband found my son dead in our garage at 4:45 p.m.

The last time I talked to Anthony was at 1:51 p.m. that afternoon when he called me asking if he could use my car when I got back home. Just that morning he told me he wanted to come back to the Church. He wanted to use my car to go and talk to our priest at the parish. I told my husband that I thought Anthony was getting better and everything was going to be okay. I was full of hope that finally he was going to come back to me.

When I got home, he was nowhere to be found and I assumed his fiancée had picked him up. Little did I know what was on the other side of the garage wall. It never occurred to me that he would have taken his own life.

Everything that happened after my husband found Anthony went fast but also in slow motion. I walked past the open garage door and could see the outline of my son's body. I first thought of keeping his manner of death to myself because I was scared of what people would think, but with the grace of God I decided that I was not going to ever be ashamed of my son. I would be angry, sad, depressed, and confused, but I would not allow myself to even consider being ashamed.

THE CHURCH PRAYS FOR MY SON'S SOUL

From the minute that we found Anthony, I knew I needed the help of my priests to pray for his soul—not because he took his own life but because praying for the dead is a huge part of our faith. So my pastor, Fr. Dean, was the first phone call I made after calling 911. He was right behind the ambulance. Fr. Jonathan, the priest who had baptized Anthony and all my kids and had walked with me through my conversion, was right behind Fr. Dean. Fr. Jonathan waited with us until the police allowed us to bless Anthony's body. He had been with me through a lot by this point, but this was by far the hardest thing either one of us had faced.

Anthony had four priests concelebrate his funeral Mass. Fr. Jonathan was so very understanding and considerate. As part of the preparations for Anthony's funeral he asked me what we would like him to say in the homily. I told him I wanted it to be a testimony of God's love for all of us and that in no way was Anthony's suicide a part of God's plan for his life. Fr. Jonathan did a great job at making those things clear. Because he had been the one to baptize Anthony and bless Anthony's body, the love he had for Anthony came through in his homily, which was a beautiful gift of love for the rest of us.

People from all over the world were praying for my son's soul. Jennifer Ful-wiler, who hosts a radio show on the Catholic Channel on SiriusXM radio, spoke about the loss of Anthony to her international audience. Jen's request for prayers for us, along with many other Catholic friends who also requested prayers for Anthony in the days after his suicide, led to an outpouring of love and prayers.

This led to such great love in me for my Church and for all the kind people who make up the Body of Christ. It also made me grateful for the many ways that we as Catholics can offer prayers for people who are suffering, including through the use of social media. People started tagging me in pictures of candles they lit for Anthony all over the place. In the days, months, and year that I could not bring myself to pray, total strangers praying for me kept me connected to God and to Anthony.

In the weeks that followed Anthony's death, many priests who are close to us reached out to help us through that terrible time. One priest blessed the garage. Fr. Jonathan prayed with us as though he was part of our family. Another priest came over and blessed St. Benedict medals to put around our house. We picked St. Benedict medals because I knew that my entire family would need all the help we could get to stay strong in the months and years to come. St. Benedict was a saint who did not fear anything because he trusted God completely.

Another priest, who had been at our parish for a while and was now a pastor of a different parish, helped me through my anger by taking time out of his busy life to have a phone conversation with me. A priest from Canada and a friend of mine through social media had been praying for Anthony in Rome in the days leading up to Anthony's suicide. Added to the prayers of all these priests, who have continued to pray for my family and offer up Masses for Anthony, were the hundreds of Mass cards and perpetual enrollments that began to flood in through the mail.

CUSSING OUT AND QUESTIONING GOD

Despite all this help, for the next year I was very angry. One of the first things I did was go to Mass and kneel in front of the tabernacle, cussing out God. Then I stopped going to Mass, I stopped praying, and I strongly considered leaving Catholicism altogether. I had prayed so hard for my son and God just sat there and watched as he took his own life. Things went wrong all the time, and this was one time that it would have been helpful for something to break, like the beam or the rope that my son hanged himself with, so that my son's life could be saved. But it didn't!

I saw a news story shortly after Anthony's suicide where a boy was saved from a fast-moving current. His mother was on the news and said, "God must have a purpose for his life to have saved him," and I threw a glass at the TV. If that were true, if God had saved that boy because he had a purpose for that kid's life, then did God not have a purpose for my son's life? How do we explain that? How do we say "thank God" when someone's kid does not die when other people's sons are dying? What is the point of praying if God was just going to let people kill themselves anyway?

I also questioned if maybe I didn't pray the right way. I have heard of miracles where God brings children back to life after they have been dead for a while and that made me wonder about my son. Was his life not worth it?

For the first year after Anthony's suicide, I had a hard time praying at all, other than to tell God that his plan sucked and that I hated it. I cried for my son, and I hoped he was in heaven. But I also wondered, if that was the way to heaven, why should any of us not follow in his footsteps? I went into a deep depression. I truly believe now that what kept me alive were the prayers of everyone who loved me and my family.

That first year was extremely difficult for me. Our priests, our friends, and my therapist have stood with me in the darkest grief. I had my own mental health issues going on and fortunately I was seeing a therapist to help me with my grief. In the midst of this, my grandbaby was having panic attacks, my husband was struggling silently, and my other kids were having nightmares and other troubling issues. We were all devastated, and I was so very angry with God.

SLOWLY CAME HEALING AND THE RETURN OF HOPE

Eventually, though, I began to see that making peace with God was the only way I was going to survive. I began to pray a little here and there after the first anniversary of Anthony's suicide. Slowly I started going back to Mass. At first I was just sitting there seething with rage, but eventually I was able to pay attention during Mass and listen to what God was saying to me.

It was at Mass that I was able to lay my heart out in the open. It was where I could talk to God about how broken I was and ask him to heal me. At daily Mass I sat in front of a painting depicting St. Rafael saying, "Before long, God will heal you," and I kept begging God for that moment. I began to read the daily readings and to keep a journal. I continue those spiritual disciplines and read the Bible regularly. These practices help me to feel stronger and stronger.

It was more than two years after we found Anthony dead in the garage before I finally felt as if God had, in fact, healed me just a little. Now I can breathe. I can pray. I can go to Mass and feel the grace of God. It is still not perfect, but I know that God loves me. I know that God loves Anthony.

The grief is still there, and it is just as painful, if not more painful, the further I get from having last seen my son alive. It is still difficult for me to watch videos of Anthony and to hear his voice. I see his children growing up knowing that they will not know him.

But even with all that, I have hope again—hope that I can tell Anthony's story. I will let people know that suicide is something we all must face as a society for the sake of our children. I have hope that I can be happy and not forget my son or leave him behind. And more than anything, I have begun to do the things I enjoy doing and live my life.

LETTING GOD INTO OUR SUFFERING

Our Catholic faith shines in the darkness. Our Catholic faith helps us endure the grief and suffering. We talk about suffering so much. We pray the Stations of the Cross to remember Christ's suffering. The saints have written volumes on how to allow God into our suffering so that it is redeemed. Reading their writings consoled me and helped me to let God into my suffering.

Through prayer I was able to see light when it was nowhere to be found. I would not have ever gotten to this place without my faith. Never.

KEY POINTS

- Suicide happens in the families of many "good" Catholics.
- Catholics need their priests, deacons, and bishops to understand, show great compassion, and come immediately to their side when a loved one dies by suicide.
- Catholics need the help of clergy and other leaders in planning the funeral after suicide takes a loved one. Their wishes regarding what a homilist preaches must be respected.
- The whole Church community ought to be encouraged to console those who experience the death of a loved one by suicide, offering comfort, prayer, and other assistance.
- Suicide and the death of a child change a person's relationship with God in ways that are distinctive. Church leaders must learn about, respect, and support the individual spiritual journey of each person who loses a loved one to suicide.
- People can, and many do, find healing and live in hope after a suicide. Church leaders must assist them in this process as companions and compassionate guides.

ASK YOURSELF

1. When there is a suicide, what can I do to reassure a Catholic family and other loved ones of the deceased that they did not fail?
2. Am I prepared to be with a family or other loved ones immediately after a suicide? In what ways? If I don't feel prepared, what will I do to be closer to ready?
3. Is my parish community prepared to openly pray for a family when there is a suicide? If not, how might I help all of us be ready for this?
4. What will I do to compassionately accompany a family through their grief, anger, and questioning of God after a suicide?
5. What will I say and do to help a family and others heal and find hope again?

5.

Priests, Suicide, and Redemption

Msgr. Stephen J. Rossetti
Diocese of Syracuse

SHARING OUR DARKNESS

It can be jarring to hear of a priest who has died by suicide. If there is anyone who should be immune to such tragedies, it ought to be a priest, a man of faith—or so we tend to think. But, sadly, there have been several priests in my recent memory who have taken their own lives.

As a priest-psychologist who has worked with priests suffering from mental health problems, I have counseled a number of priests who have been suicidal. Thankfully, few actually died by suicide, but some did. Each one we lost was a searing tragedy for all of us who were assisting him. As mental health professionals, we inquire if our clients are suicidal, particularly if there are troublesome signs. We have tests to measure the extent and lethality of one's suicidality. But men, especially, are not always honest about such feelings and may keep them hidden. They know what will happen if they admit to being seriously suicidal, which includes ending up in a locked psychiatric unit.

Moreover, it is difficult for many men to admit having such distressing feelings. They are usually ashamed of these feelings, and they feel weak and vulnerable. Many do not like to reach out for help and instead typically carry their burdens alone, which only makes their situations worse and the danger of actual suicide more acute.

This can be especially true of priests, given their role as faith leaders and shepherds. As the psychologist Dr. Melinda Moore commented in the wake of the suicide of a Missouri priest in 2020, "Priests are no different from the rest of us. The difference is that priests and other clergy oftentimes are idealized and held to a standard where they feel as if they can't ask for help. They are the individuals that other people come to for help, and so they themselves feel they can't seek help."[1]

Perhaps in our education of people in general and priests in particular, we can do a better job of emphasizing the importance of sharing suicidal feelings with others. We need to tell people it is okay to have such feelings and that many of the people around them want to help. They need to know that hiding these dark emotions only makes it worse.

AN INTERNAL "HELL"

In addition to working with priests and religious in psychological distress, I also teach pastoral courses to seminarians. When we get to the module on mood disorders, I tell them point-blank, "If you are depressed enough, you *will* consider suicide." This is universally true. A real depression carries with it an internal pain that can become excruciating as the depression increases. In these situations, the thought of taking one's own life occurs spontaneously. The seriously depressed person is in a lot of internal pain and desperately wants to get out of it. Sometimes suicide can seem like the only option. A depressed person shared that she was having thoughts of killing herself. A well-meaning Catholic friend replied to her, "You don't want to kill yourself. You will go to hell." The depressed woman responded, "I am already in hell."

I have known or been aware of several priests who have died by suicide in recent memory after long struggles with depression and mental difficulties. Typically, their parish communities were shocked by the loss because the priest's illness was kept hidden. Few knew of his depression and interior struggle. On the outside, these men often seemed fine and generously served the needs of their people.

Our Catholic faith has been, for many, a deterrent to taking one's own life. It offers hope in a loving God and an admonition against such an act. This is a good thing. But when depression and shame take over one's consciousness, the darkness can push out the light. Even for priests, the notion that there is a loving, merciful God can recede into the distance in the midst of such an excruciating darkness.

I shudder to think about what will happen in our world as secularism spreads and the image of a loving, forgiving God vanishes altogether from many people's minds. Suicide rates in many countries, including the United States, are rising.

The Centers for Disease Control and Prevention reported that the suicide rate in the US increased by one-third since 1999.[2] As secularism spreads, I wonder if suicide rates will continue to rise.

But even for those who have faith as a resource, we need to recognize the internal "hell" that some people are living in and do what we can to help. For them, the internal pain can become so overwhelming as to blind their mind's eye to any source of hope. Perhaps the first thing we can do is try to *create an open, sharing environment* where people feel free to share their darkest feelings and discuss openly mental illnesses and the toll they take on one's well-being. Yet we realize that, in their internal hell, some will simply emotionally shut down and not be able to communicate their pain, their hell, to anyone.

UNLOVABLE AND UNFORGIVABLE

Some of the priests who took their own lives did so in the wake of accusations of having abused a minor. Priests are typically seen as holy or at least good people. They are representatives of the Church and of God, ordained to act *in persona Christi capitis*, in the person of Christ the head. This is a persona that priests typically believe of themselves. They perceive themselves as good people trying to help others. When allegations of having abused a minor surface, this persona is destroyed and the truth of their despicable sins surfaces. The cognitive dissonance, in the consciousness of such priests, between being a good priest and being an evil child molester is overwhelming. The world now sees them as child molesters, and they have to face the awful truth and public shame. It can be an unbearable weight, and many of them feel that the world would be better off without them. In 2002, in the wake of the Church child abuse scandal that erupted in Boston and spread throughout the country, more than a dozen accused priests ended their own lives.

This is an extreme scenario, but the basic, underlying dynamics have some similarities to many others who die by suicide. Some people who take their own lives believe that they are not lovable; they may feel that their own failures and sins are unforgivable; some have lost hope in themselves and in their future. When they look at themselves, they often see only darkness, hopelessness, and self-worthlessness. They believe they are a burden and the world would be better off without them.

Suicidal people often feel unlovable and unforgivable. Sadly, this message is communicated to people in many different ways. Those who are orphaned at birth often struggle with feeling rejected and somehow less than others. Individuals who have committed serious crimes and sins will likely struggle as well. "Am I lovable? Can I be forgiven?" These are fundamental human questions buried deep in such people's hearts and I suspect in every person's heart. This is the universal human quest for redemption. "Can I be saved? Will I be loved and saved by the One who can save me?"

We know that Satan tempts all of us to sin and to commit acts against life. The Evil One's message to us is a negative message of condemnation and death. Evil whispers in our ears: "You are worthless." "God doesn't care about you." "You can never be forgiven." "There is no hope for you." "You belong to us." "Take your own life." While Satan cannot force us to kill ourselves, his evil voice can tempt us to do so, sometimes incessantly.

FINDING LOVE, HEALING, AND FORGIVENESS

None of us are immune to these kinds of dark thoughts, which never come from God. Such dark thoughts often emerge from mental illness and/or the dark part of a soul not yet fully redeemed in Christ. Satan tries to exploit our vulnerabilities and echoes his message of death inside our heads. Thus it is often helpful to engage in healing mental health therapies as well as spiritual healing, including the Sacrament of Penance, healing prayers, and regular attendance at Eucharist. But the journey to full and complete healing is a long one, and often difficult to navigate.

A young woman who is fervent in her practice of the Catholic faith shared her story with me. Born in Eastern Europe, she was placed in an orphanage at birth and sometime later she was adopted by an American family. Throughout her formative years she struggled with depression and suicidality. She could not shake the feeling of isolation and internal pain, the feeling of being unloved and forgotten. "What happened?" I asked. She explained that while she was in college, she came to know the Lord personally. Faith came alive for her and she felt God's personal love and healing. As a result of her faith experiences, she has not been suicidal or greatly depressed for some years now. She continues to struggle in many ways, but she has turned the corner on her suicidal past. She credits the grace of God and I would add the loving Catholic community that clearly surrounds us. As she spoke to me, there were two women next to her that obviously loved and supported her.

Like the young woman who was orphaned, God sometimes speaks directly to a person's soul. When God whispers in our ear, he tells us, "You are loved. You are forgiven. Come to me and I will heal you. I have prepared a place of joy and peace for you. In Jesus, you are saved." God revealed directly to her that she was indeed loved, healed, and forgiven.

But most often God works through others. It is we who must communicate his message of love, healing, and forgiveness. Ours are often the voices he uses and the arms that communicate his love and welcoming embrace.

THE UNIVERSAL NEED FOR REDEMPTION

For the priest who struggles with depression, we spontaneously want to be God's loving arms and his forgiving voice. For the priest who has molested minors, this is a great challenge. An older priest in Germany gave a homily in 2019 in which he said we need to forgive priests who molest minors. He could not finish the homily because he was booed and shouted down by the congregation. I certainly understand their reaction. It seems impossible to think of forgiving their despicable and horrible crimes—evils that we can never tolerate or minimize.

What about terrorists? Should we forgive those who blew up the World Trade Center in New York City on 9/11? Thousands of people died. The suffering brought about by such evil was, and continues to be, immense.

I am reminded of Pope John Paul II, now sainted, who went into Rebibbia prison in Rome and personally forgave the terrorist Ali Ağca, who shot him four times. And again, St. Maria Goretti who, at the age of eleven, was stabbed fourteen times by Alessandro. She would not give in to his sexual advances. She died shortly thereafter, forgiving Alessandro and expressing the desire that he be with her in heaven. He repented. After his prison sentence, Alessandro attended the canonization ceremony with Maria's mother. He became and died as a lay brother with the Capuchin Franciscans. These are examples of a forgiving, redemptive love.

I am told by exorcists that they cannot hate the demons that they are exorcizing, even if only in their hearts. They say that the demons feed off the hatred and it slows, if not halts, the liberation. Demons commit their despicable acts in an attempt to make us just like them—full of hatred and violence. Terrorists unwittingly try to foster in our hearts that same evil hatred that spurred their actions.

If our forgiveness is conditional, then it is not God's forgiveness we are offering. Perhaps we have a hard time forgiving those most despised among us because we do not understand what real forgiveness means. It does not mean a person should not be imprisoned for one's crimes; both Ali Ağca and Alessandro went to prison. It does not mean we approve or support in any way their evil actions. It does not mean that we cannot feel a righteous anger against such evil. But it does mean we, like St. Maria Goretti and St. John Paul II, want what is best for them. Maria and John Paul desired and prayed that these criminals would be converted, know the redemption of Christ, and be received into the kingdom. We are called to do the same, in the name of Christ's redeeming love. If we can bring ourselves as a Church and as individuals to speak and live forgiveness to even those who commit horrendous evil, we will show them the love of God and even they will hopefully find the light.

JUSTICE FILLED WITH MERCY

We do not know the final fate of those who take their own lives, just as we do not know the final fate of any who die (except for the saints, whom the Church proclaims are in heaven). But we do know that our God always stands ready and continually invites all of us to forgiveness and life. I preached at the memorial Mass of a priest who died by suicide. I told the congregation that we cannot judge this man, because judgment belongs to God. "Does God judge a person's life by one single act? Is his life to be summed up in that one act?" As we looked at his life, there were many acts of kindness toward others. He had been a priest for others again and again. A true act of love can never be forgotten.

Sadly, some priests do die by suicide. We can help prevent some of those who are suicidal from committing the final act by surrounding them with communities of loving forgiveness and support for those who struggle with mental illness. We can and ought to invite them to share their dark feelings and to reach out to others for help and support. They learn about God's healing love most often through us.

But other suicides we cannot prevent. Their suicidality sometimes remains hidden and their hopelessness and inner pain overwhelm their consciousness. Some have struggled with their dark feelings for years, perhaps most of their lives. They are worn out from struggling again and again. For them, suicide feels like the only way out. We pray for them, we love them, and we forgive them if they harm us. We recognize that God is the true and ultimate judge and his justice is permeated by mercy. If we can love and forgive someone, no matter the darkness to which they have succumbed, I do not believe that God can and will do any less.

KEY POINTS

• Anyone can be vulnerable to suicidal ideation, even priests and other religious leaders, particularly if they are suffering from mental illness, especially depression.

- Depression and mental illness can make a person feel like they are living in hell. In their internal hell, some will emotionally shut down and not communicate their pain to anyone.
- Some people feel that they are unlovable and unforgivable, and the world would be better off without them.
- We need to create open, sharing environments where people can find the courage to share their darkest feelings.
- God always offers hope, love, healing, and forgiveness and will work through us to help people learn about his healing love.

ASK YOURSELF

1. Am I prepared to acknowledge and discuss how mental illness, depression, and suicide affect ministers in the Church?
2. Can ministers and leaders in my Catholic community accept that they may at times need mental health care and treatment? If not, what can I do to remedy this?
3. How do I feel about offering forgiveness, love, and hope, even to a criminal or someone who has committed a heinous act?
4. How can I communicate God's mercy to the families and other loved ones of a person who has died by suicide?

PART II.

CHURCH TEACHING ON SUICIDE

What It Says and What It Doesn't

6.

Extending the Church's Compassion to Survivors of Suicide

Archbishop Wilton Gregory
Archdiocese of Washington, DC

Fr. Charles T. Rubey is a cherished priest friend of mine with nearly fifty years of distinguished service to Catholic Charities of the Archdiocese of Chicago. Fr. Rubey mentioned to me that he knew of several shameful incidents of people grieving the loss of loved ones to suicide being insensitively treated by priests rather than being comforted. Some had actually been told that their loved one was in hell because of their suicide.

The sorrow that every person feels as they lament the loss of a loved one in death is universal, and the Church is in an irreplaceable position of comforting people in the name of Christ at that moment—not shaming them with cruel comments that only intensify their grief. During his five decades at Catholic Charities, Fr. Rubey has dealt with countless suicides, murders, and violent deaths of all types. He founded the Loving Outreach to Survivors of Suicide (LOSS) program at Catholic Charities of Chicago to help support and comfort people facing the unimaginable pain of a tragic self-inflicted death of a loved one or friend. (Fr. Rubey writes about the LOSS program in chapter 14.)

Oftentimes our news is filled with sad reports of prominent people who have taken their own lives. Such high-profile tragedies drive home the fact that we are all subject to personal and professional trials, no matter our public personas or status in life. We know that mental health is a serious societal concern that does not discriminate based on wealth or influence, yet those of us of more moderate means are often puzzled when affluent people succumb to their despondency. We wrongly assume that success and riches alleviate sadness and suffering, or at the very least guarantee the privileged access to the finest professional care to address feelings of despair. That is clearly not the case. Hopelessness is an equal opportunity destroyer of souls.

Human life is precious and inviolable, as our Church consistently teaches. It is always appalling when human life is destroyed through abortion, war, capital punishment, euthanasia, or blatant disregard for the human rights and dignity of the poor. Those who are severely depressed, live with a psychological disorder, or struggle with mental illness cannot at times make sound judgments and therefore may not be culpable in destroying or even ending their own lives.

Only God can know and judge the heart of someone who takes his or her own life. Only God can know the state of the soul of a person who has reached the end of their emotional capacities. While the Church's teaching on suicide underscores its gravity, our compassion must always be extended to those who lose a loved one to suicide (*CCC*, 2283).

Life offers all of us many painful moments, and at times these may seem insurmountable. The importance of family, faith, and friends cannot be overemphasized when confronting the difficulties that inevitably come our way. We probably all know of a family—perhaps even our own—that has faced a violent loss of a loved one. They need our compassionate outreach. The Church, above all, must be the community that seeks to comfort, console, and support people in those moments of tragedy. We violate the very image of Christ when we dare to make judgments that belong only to the merciful heart of the Father.

My conversation with Fr. Rubey reminded me of how we clergy are offered the immense privilege of healing and comforting the grieving in the very figure of Christ as we console those who have lost a loved one—no matter what the circumstances. Our words and attitudes must reflect those of the Lord who came as the reflection of the Father's mercy. With humble hearts, we must leave the final judgment of such drastic actions to God alone, "for his mercy endures forever" (Ps 136).

KEY POINTS

- The Church is in an irreplaceable position of comforting people in the name of Christ—not shaming them with cruel comments that only intensify their grief.

- While the Church's teaching on suicide underscores its gravity, our compassion must always be extended to those who lose a loved one to suicide.
- Our words and attitudes must reflect those of the Lord who came as the reflection of the Father's mercy.

ASK YOURSELF

1. How can I ensure that I am prepared to offer unconditional compassionate support, free of any judgment, to a person who is grieving a suicide?
2. Do I understand Church teaching on suicide well enough to confidently reassure those who are grieving a suicide of God's mercy? If not, what will I do to help strengthen my understanding?

7.

History and Pastoral Practice of Catholic Teaching on Suicide

Archbishop Salvatore J. Cordileone
Archdiocese of San Francisco

It is altogether unlawful to kill oneself. . . .
Hence, suicide is always a mortal sin, as being contrary to the natural law and to charity.

—*Summa Theologica*, 2a-2ae q. 64, a. 5

Grave psychological disturbances, anguish, or grave fear of hardship, suffering, or torture can diminish the responsibility of the one committing suicide. We should not despair of the eternal salvation of persons who have taken their own lives.

—*Catechism of the Catholic Church*, 2282–2283

A "GRAVE MATTER"

Suicide, the deliberate action or lack of action taken to result in one's own death, has long been condemned in most of the Western world, with its Judeo-Christian heritage. In recent years, however, we have seen a steady increase in the number of suicides, and our recent popes have frequently warned of a culture of death, which continues to exert an ever-increasing influence on popular culture. A study released by the Centers for Disease Control and Prevention in 2018 showed a 30 percent increase in suicides—across all races, age groups, and both sexes—in the United States since 2000. Euthanasia is now legal in seven states and the District of Columbia, and the high-profile assisted-suicide death of Brittany Maynard in 2014 prompted renewed interest in the topic.

What is the understanding of the Catholic Church regarding suicide? The nineteenth-century French positivist philosopher Auguste Comte claimed that the eternal glory of Catholicism was that it did not permit suicide for any reason.[1] Catholicism and Islam are the only religions with a long history of vigorous opposition to suicide. According to the Angelic Doctor, St. Thomas Aquinas, suicide is a mortal sin; therefore, by definition, it "causes exclusion from Christ's kingdom and the eternal death of hell" (*CCC*, 1861).

Suicide has always been considered a grave matter and unlawful by the Church, since it presumes authority over life (which only God has). It is also a supreme offense against the charity that each person owes to one's own self, depriving oneself of the greatest good in one's possession—one's own life—and thwarting the possibility of arriving at the realization of one's ultimate purpose in life. It can also be a source of grave scandal (*CCC*, 2282). The previous (1917) Code of Canon Law legislated deprivation of Christian burial to those who took their own lives ("*qui se ipsi occiderint deliberato consilio*" [can. 1240, sec. 1, n. 3]).

In modern times, however, there has been an acknowledgment of the many extenuating factors that may influence or induce a person to suicide. The current (1983) Code of Canon Law, in fact, does not mention suicide in the list of those who are to be deprived of ecclesiastical funerals (can. 1184), although it also acknowledges the gravity of the matter by maintaining attempted suicide as an irregularity to receiving Holy Orders (can. 1041, n. 5). This brief chapter will summarize Catholic understanding and treatment of suicide as it has developed and as it exists today.

SUICIDE AND THEOLOGICAL PRINCIPLES

Suicide consists of an action that either directly or indirectly causes one's own death. The morality of any act is determined by three things: the *end* or intention of the act, the *object* or means by which it is accomplished, and the *circumstances* surrounding the act. We also have the *principle of double effect*, whereby a morally good or neutral end is obtained through means that also have an objectively bad result, as long as certain conditions are met. To determine the morality of an act of suicide, there are as well four aspects that must be considered: it is either direct or indirect and either positive or negative.

Suicide is termed *direct* when a person has the intention of causing his or her own death, either as an end in itself or as a means to another end such as escaping physical pain, disgrace, or ruin. The last is more common. St. Thérèse of Lisieux, for example, suffered such pain from tuberculosis at the end of her life that she is reported to have said, "If I didn't have faith, I could never bear such suffering. I am surprised that there aren't more suicides among atheists."[2] She also reportedly asked her mother superior to move her bottle of pain pills out of arm's reach, so that she would not be tempted to take them and end her life through an overdose. In itself, suicide is always morally evil.

Indirect suicide occurs when a person does not desire his or her own death, either as an end in itself or as a means to another end, but commits an act that will certainly, or at least likely, have the effect of ending his or her own life. This can sometimes be an act of virtue, in which case it usually would not be considered suicide per se, even though it does result in one's own death. Samson's killing of the Philistines, which cost his own life, would be an example (Jgs 16:23–30). St. Damien's work in the leper colony of Molokai, which resulted in his own death from leprosy, would be another.

These latter two are examples of *positive* causes of (indirect) suicide, since death in each case results from actions taken by the individual. *Negative* causes of suicide occur when an individual fails or chooses not to take an action necessary for the individual's survival. Some early Christian ascetics who essentially died of starvation could fall into this category. A modern-day example of negative indirect suicide could be refusing extraordinary means of medical intervention (the Church does not require accepting such extreme medical intervention). Generally speaking, when suicide is considered, we are referring to direct actions taken that result in one's death.

SUICIDE IN THE BIBLE

In his book *Suicide in Rabbinic Literature*, Rabbi Sidney Goldstein writes, "The Bible does not have an explicit prohibition against suicide."[3] In fact, according to Goldstein's study of rabbinical literature, "although suicide is viewed with the utmost severity by many authorities and often spoken of in the most condemnatory terms, there is no explicit statement in the Torah prohibiting it."[4] However, Genesis 9:6 has been interpreted as such a prohibition in the Talmud,[5] as well as certainly the fifth commandment of the Decalogue ("Thou shalt not kill"). A typical rabbinic statement that can be seen concerning those who die by suicide is "For a suicide, no rites whatever should be observed."[6]

There are six cases of suicide mentioned in the Old Testament: Samson, King Saul and his armor-bearer (1 Chr 10:4–5), Abimelech (Jgs 9:50–54), Ahithophel (2 Sm 17:23), and Razis (2 Mc 14:37–46). However, Samson's action is considered an act of warfare, not a suicide, while the others have various potentially extenuating circumstances, according to different rabbinic commentators.

As the Jewish community has wrestled with these cases (and others) over the years, there has been an apparent reluctance to condemn any but directly intended, positive suicide, done for its own sake. Indeed, a review of contemporary rabbinic literature suggests that currently, "the culpability of any suicide has been reduced almost to the point of being nonexistent."[7] This is due to a variety of factors, the primary ones being (1) a "requirement . . . [of a] statement prior to a suicide attempt to establish intention";[8] and (2) the recognition that suicide is, by its very nature, an irrational act. This accords with Christian moral theology, that if the end of an act is neither directly intended nor capable of being rationally intended to be evil, subjective culpability is diminished or removed.

SUICIDE IN THE ROMAN EMPIRE

In pagan Greece and early Rome there was no prohibition against suicide; free men had the right to take their own lives for a variety of reasons, particularly for the sake of "honor."[9] In fact, among the intellectual elite it was often lauded, particularly among the Cynics and the Stoics, who considered it "the highest expression of liberty," such that it was not infrequently carried out publicly with witnesses, almost theatrically.[10] Pliny the Elder claimed that suicide was "the greatest advantage [God] has given man among all the great drawbacks of life."[11] During the time of the Roman Empire, the rate of suicide increased dramatically, and it was so common it was referred to as the "Roman death."[12]

This began to change in the Roman Empire, as suicide—and especially, the increasing incidents of it among slaves—was seen to weaken the economic well-being of the imperium, the supreme executive power of the Roman state. The true change, however, came with St. Augustine, who was prompted in part to respond to the effects of Constantine and a Christianity that was no longer oppressed, and the Donatist heresy.

SUICIDE IN EARLY CHRISTIANITY AND THE WRITING OF ST. AUGUSTINE

In the early years of Christianity, with frequent persecutions, martyrdom was not uncommon. Early Christian writers such as Ignatius, Polycarp, and John Chrysostom, as well as Eusebius, could be seen as encouraging willing submission to death for pious reasons as a worthy goal for Christians.[13] The Donatist heresy took this to an extreme, encouraging their followers to antagonize both pagans and (non-Donatist) Christians to kill them, seeing martyrdom as a quick path to heaven.

In response, St. Augustine declared a clear position against suicide, stating that it was "a detestable crime and a damnable wickedness."[14] His defense of the prohibition was based not only on the fifth commandment but also rational arguments: (1) to take one's own life was to take onto oneself an act that only the state or Church had the right to authorize; (2) to escape the sufferings of the world was not only weak and therefore ignoble and unworthy of a Christian but also a failure to "suffer for Christ's sake"; and (3) to kill oneself in order to avoid future sin—as some heretical newly baptized Christians were doing—was a greater sin than any that might be potentially committed.[15]

At the time, suicide was considered by many as a defense of a woman's honor, given that killing oneself was seen by many as more honorable than submitting to rape. Against this, Augustine wrote that those who had been violated were, in fact, still chaste, since the act was committed against their will (the title of chapter 16 of *The City of God*, book 1, is "Violation of Chastity, without the Will's Consent, Cannot Pollute the Character"). However, when discussing the famous case of Lucretia, a young Roman woman who had been raped and then died by her own hand, he stated that by committing suicide she had committed a greater sin. In other words, suicide was no longer to be considered honorable.

Over time, Augustine's position that suicide was always murder became clearly established as the official teaching of the Church. Augustine wrote, "For it is clear that if no one has a private right to kill even a guilty man (and no law allows this), then certainly anyone who kills himself is a murderer."[16] The Council of Braga in 563, for example, prohibited funerals for those who died by suicide, while the 1284 Synod of Nimes refused them burial in a consecrated cemetery. The acceptance of this prohibition against suicide by Christendom can be seen by noting that between AD 400 and 1400 there were very few notable suicides among orthodox Christians.[17]

SUICIDE IN THE MIDDLE AGES AND THE WRITING OF ST. THOMAS AQUINAS

St. Thomas, writing in the thirteenth century, methodically developed St. Augustine's work as he formed what has remained the basis for Christian thought on most topics to this day. Writing of suicide in a more philosophical approach than St. Augustine, he stated that suicide was "unnatural" (since the will to live is among the strongest instincts of all living creatures) and thus opposed to the will of God. It is also a sin against charity toward self, since it deprives oneself of the greatest good one possesses. Further, it results in removing oneself from the community of which we are all a part—thus an act of violation of the good of the community. Finally, and perhaps most critical, we all belong to God, in a very real sense, and so to take one's own life is to take what belongs to God alone and is therefore an act of direct ill will toward the Creator.[18] St. Thomas's writings, as noted, have influenced all Catholic thought since then; his contemporary Dante Alighieri puts those who died by suicide somewhere below heretics and murderers in his *Inferno*.

SUICIDE, THE RENAISSANCE, AND REFORMATION

As with all else, the advent of the Reformers, the Renaissance, and the Enlightenment affected the common understanding of suicide. John Calvin's theology of predestination, for example, brought the question of culpability of death by suicide into question: If a person was predestined to damnation, what difference would suicide make? Although Calvin did include suicide among the list of sins Christians should avoid.

While Reformist theology generally condemned suicide, the concept of autonomy and self-determination as the greatest good came to be accepted more broadly in society, and the generally accepted prohibition against suicide began to weaken. The word *suicide* itself was coined in 1642, indicating a perhaps more positive action, over against the term *self-killing*, which had been used by the Christian Church.[19] In thirty-two of Shakespeare's plays, for example, twenty-four characters die by suicide, many for "noble" reasons.[20] Among secular rationalist reformers, Erasmus, Montesquieu, and Jean-Jacques Rousseau all considered suicide a reasonable, even at times laudable option; Rousseau claimed that one should "do whatever you conceive to be for your own good, provided you thereby do no injury to others,"[21] a philosophy often echoed in our contemporary culture.

SUICIDE AT THE END OF THE NINETEENTH CENTURY

At the close of the nineteenth century, Christian rulers still condemned suicide and called for strong civil penalties. However, the Christian worldview no longer held universal sway. Laws against suicide began to relax at the end of the Renaissance, and the traditional Latin Christian prohibitions of Christian burial were relaxed or abolished in many places.[22]

With the traditional teaching against the commission of suicide swept away by the Rationalists, the Romantics elevated suicide to a noble endeavor (we see this echoed in the modern-day support for Brittany Maynard's suicide and in arguments for the legalization of euthanasia). In response, more stringent secular measures against suicide were adopted, particularly in France, but with mixed success.[23]

By the close of the nineteenth century, this would be a good summary of Christian thought on suicide:

> The Old Testament of the Western world does not directly forbid suicide, but in Jewish law suicide is wrong. During the early Christian years, there was excessive martyrdom, i.e., suicide, resulting in considerable concern on the part of the Church Fathers. St. Augustine (354–430 AD) categorically rejected suicide. Suicide was considered a sin because it violated the sixth [*sic*] Commandment, "Thou shalt not kill". By 693 AD, the Church of the Council of Toledo proclaimed that individuals who attempted suicide should be excommunicated. St. Thomas Aquinas (1225–1274) espoused suicide to be a grave mortal sin. The notion of suicide as sin took firm hold in the West for hundreds of years. Only during the Renaissance and the Reformation did a different view emerge.[24]

THE TWENTIETH CENTURY AND INSIGHTS OF MODERN SOCIOLOGY AND PSYCHOLOGY

It is impossible to overstate the effects of modern sociology and psychology on the understanding of human nature. The study of suicide as a sociological phenomenon was first accomplished in a methodological manner by the French sociologist Émile Durkheim in his 1897 volume *Suicide*, which concluded, among other things, that higher rates of religious belief led to lower rates of suicide (which he attributed to the "social integration" factor of religion—those more integrated into the fabric of a society were less likely to die by suicide).

Probably more importantly, the psychoanalyst Sigmund Freud presaged a revolution in the understanding of the human person with his theories on the makeup of the human mind, with its id, ego, and superego. Traditionally, suicide had been held to result from the influence of demons, particularly through the "use" of three of the "negative emotions" (from which came the seven deadly sins): anger, sloth, and sadness.[25] While not discounting the actions of demons, we now understand to a far greater degree the complexity of the human mind, psychological and psychiatric pathologies, and the effects they can have in human decision-making. Pathological mental conditions can be of both psychic and physical origin, and can reduce or remove the volitional decision-making ability of those whom they afflict.

Cultural, social, political, hereditary, psychological, and psychiatric factors have all influenced the occurrence of suicide and the rates of suicide in individuals and human populations.[26] While Catholics are influenced by all these factors, we are called to be "in the world, not of the world" and thus to resist those external influences that come from a "culture of death." However, psychological and psychiatric factors are usually outside of voluntary control. The Church recognizes this and notes in the *Catechism of the Catholic Church* that mental illness or distress can diminish one's responsibility in taking one's own life (*CCC*, 2282).

CHANGES IN CANON LAW REGARDING A CATHOLIC BURIAL

Up until recently, Catholics were taught that "persons who willingly and knowingly commit such an act die in a state of mortal sin and are deprived of Christian burial" (*Baltimore Catechism*, q. 1274). However, as mentioned above, the current Code of Canon Law has removed this restriction, given the Church's recognition that the state of a person's culpability for suicide may be mitigated or removed by circumstances. Only those who manifest a public repudiation of the Church, such as "those who chose the cremation of their bodies for reasons contrary to Christian faith" (can. 1184, sec. 1, n. 2) must be refused Christian burial.

EUTHANASIA AND ASSISTED SUICIDE

In our day, rationales for suicide, and particularly for the assisted suicide movement, have their roots in philosophies of preceding centuries: Stoicism (that one should have absolute power over one's fate); Epicureanism (that life is only meaningful if pleasurable); Rationalism (that arguments against suicide are based on irrational "superstition"); Romanticism (a self-directed death is preferable to the cruelty of terminal illness and pain); and "irrationalism" (that rational attempts to preserve life are unwanted interference into personal autonomy, which thus places an irrational belief in the supreme goodness of self-determination).[27]

Over against this, we have the consistent teaching of the Church—always and everywhere—on the objective grave evil of suicide. One more recent authentic source of this teaching is the *Declaration on Euthanasia* issued by the Congregation for the Doctrine of the Faith in 1980, which states:

- No one can make an attempt on the life of an innocent person, without committing a crime of the utmost gravity.
- Everyone has the duty to lead his or her life in accordance with God's plan, [which] finds its full perfection only in eternal life.
- Intentionally causing one's own death, or suicide, is therefore equally as wrong as murder; such an action on the part of a person is to be considered as a rejection of God's sovereignty and loving plan. Furthermore, suicide is also often a refusal of love for self, the denial of the natural instinct to live, a flight from the duties of justice and charity owed to one's neighbor, to various communities, or to the whole of society.[28]

MITIGATING PSYCHOLOGICAL FACTORS AND GOD'S MERCY

While suicide is always considered a grave matter and generally prohibited, and directly intended suicide is always objectively evil, the Church presumes neither the subjective culpability nor eternal destination of those who die by suicide. Indeed, this very statement of the Sacred Congregation for the Doctrine of the Faith, in upholding the Church's time-honored teaching on the grave matter of taking one's own life, also recognizes the possibility of extenuating mitigating circumstances, for it immediately adds, "as is generally recognized, at times there are psychological factors present that can diminish responsibility or even completely remove it."

This more nuanced approach to suicide on the part of the Church is reflective of the proper sense of development of doctrine. Church teaching does not change in the sense of becoming something different from what it was; rather, over time, the Holy Spirit leads the Church in acquiring a deeper understanding of the truths of revelation. Nothing new is added to the deposit of faith, but what is implicit in it is drawn out more clearly such that the content of revelation is better understood in all of its ramifications (cf. *CCC*, 86). Consequently, the *Catechism of the Catholic Church* reaffirms this deeper understanding of suicide in acknowledging that "grave psychological disturbances, anguish, or grave fear of hardship, suffering, or torture can diminish the responsibility of the one committing suicide" (*CCC*, 2282). Accordingly, "we should not despair of the eternal salvation of persons who have taken their own lives. By ways known to him alone, God can provide the opportunity for salutary repentance. The Church prays for persons who have taken their own lives" (*CCC*, 2283).

Developments in the behavioral sciences as well as the Church's own experience in pastoral outreach to families affected by the tragedy of suicide have assisted the Church in following the guidance of the Holy Spirit to a more mature and complete understanding of this troubling phenomenon. May all such families take consolation in God's infinite mercy, so that "the peace of God that surpasses all understanding will guard [their] hearts and minds in Christ Jesus" (Phil 4:7).

KEY POINTS

- Suicide is a grave matter. The Catholic Church does not permit suicide for any reason.
- The Bible does not explicitly prohibit suicide. Church teaching on suicide has developed over time as the Church acquired a deeper understanding of suicide.
- In early Christianity, St. Augustine declared a clear position against suicide in response to those who were encouraging suicidal martyrdom to get to heaven.
- In the Middle Ages, St. Thomas Aquinas wrote that suicide was unnatural and against the will of God, who created us to live.
- During the Renaissance, resistance to suicide in society began to weaken as concepts of self-determination took hold. Yet the Church still condemned suicide and consistently teaches that euthanasia and assisted suicide are grave evils.

- In the twentieth century, new understandings of the psychological and psychiatric factors leading to suicide led the Church to affirm that such factors can diminish "the responsibility of one committing suicide."
- The *Catechism* teaches that "we should not despair of the eternal salvation of persons who have taken their own lives. By ways known to him alone, God can provide the opportunity for salutatory repentance. The Church prays for persons who have taken their own lives" (*CCC*, 2283).

ASK YOURSELF

1. What did St. Augustine and St. Thomas Aquinas teach about suicide?
2. How did modern psychology and psychiatry influence Church teaching on suicide?
3. What is the difference between what the Church teaches about refusing extraordinary means of medical intervention, euthanasia, and suicide?
4. What is God's mercy, and how does it influence our understanding of the eternal salvation of those who have died by suicide?

8.

Moral Theology and Church Teaching on Suicide

Fr. Carter Griffin
Rector of Saint John Paul II Seminary

The death of a loved one is always painful. When that death is self-inflicted, the pain is nearly unbearable. For most religious believers, the pain is further amplified by the knowledge that suicide in and of itself is morally wrong. Nevertheless, and without any contradiction, the Church accompanies with words of comfort and hope those who have lost loved ones by suicide. This chapter will explore some aspects of the Church's teaching on suicide and why spiritual encouragement can still be experienced by those facing the bitter trial of a loved one taking his or her own life.

Older Catholics may recall that, before the revision of the Code of Canon Law in 1983, a person who died by suicide would often be denied funeral rites and burial in a Catholic cemetery. Since that limitation was removed in the new Code, it is assumed by many that Catholic teaching on suicide has changed. In fact, it has not, and by understanding the reasons for the shift in liturgical and pastoral practice, we can come to a deeper understanding of the unchanged teaching of the Church while also finding solid ground for spiritual comfort for those touched by suicide.

THE ASSUMPTION OF PERSONAL RESPONSIBILITY

The earlier restrictions that the Church placed on funerals and burials had two primary motivations. The first was a keen sense of the moral seriousness of the act and the general assumption that someone who committed a sinful act was nearly always culpable—that is, personally guilty—for it. If someone died while committing a grave sin, it was reasoned, then the prayers of the Church would avail little since that individual could not be saved. It is undoubtedly true that many in the past simply assumed that those who died by suicide were lost souls. Nevertheless, I think that our ancestors in faith had a bit more nuance in their thinking than is generally believed. After all, while recognizing the reality of hell and the real possibility of going there, the Church has steadfastly refused to declare any particular individual in hell, as she does sometimes for those in heaven—namely, canonized saints.

The Church has always understood that judgment belongs to God alone and that the human conscience is ultimately inscrutable to anyone but God. As St. Paul himself said, "I do not even pass judgment on myself; I am not conscious of anything against me, but I do not thereby stand acquitted; the one who judges me is the Lord" (1 Cor 4:3–4). In fact, in the past, some who took their own lives were still given Catholic funerals when their cause of death was officially registered as mental illness or trauma rather than suicide. In one famous nineteenth-century case, Archduke Rudolf, heir to the Austro-Hungarian throne, was discovered dead with a self-inflicted wound. Suicide would have prevented him from receiving a Church funeral and being interred in the Imperial Crypt. However, he was declared to have been in a state of "mental imbalance" when he died and was permitted a Church burial. Surely such concessions were more common than a stark reading of canon law would suggest. There was less presumed certainty about a person's eternal judgment than is sometimes supposed today.

DETERRING SUICIDE

The second motive for the old restrictions on funerals and burials was more decisive. It was to limit the possibility of scandal to the faithful. *Scandal* in this context does not mean shock or outrage, as the term is generally used today. It means leading someone else into sin. When Jesus gravely warns his hearers against "causing one of these little ones who believe [in me] to sin" (Mk 9:24), the word he uses is to "*scandalize* the little ones." It was thought that withholding funeral and burial ceremonies from those who died by suicide would deter those contemplating it, thereby saving lives, and also prevent copycat suicides afterward, thus saving even more lives. As those who work with young people today can affirm, this second concern continues to be relevant. The number of schools across the country that have endured a rash of suicides in a short period of time gives ample testimony to the fact.

THE UNCHANGING TEACHING OF THE CHURCH

These two prudential judgments, then, informed the Church's previous liturgical and pastoral practice for those who took their own lives. They were pastoral decisions, embedded in canon law, reflecting both the objective teaching itself and also particular judgments concerning individual culpability and the risk of scandal—that is, the danger to others. Those pastoral considerations remain important today, and I will come back to them.

First, though, we should review the basic and unchanged teaching of the Church regarding suicide. "Everyone," the Church teaches in the *Catechism of the Catholic Church*, "is responsible for his life before God who has given it to him. It is God who remains the sovereign Master of life. We are obliged to accept life gratefully and preserve it for his honor and the salvation of our souls. We are stewards, not owners, of the life God has entrusted to us. It is not ours to dispose of" (*CCC*, 2280).

Though there are often many emotional, psychological, and even spiritual factors that may diminish our moral guilt, it is nevertheless true that in the objective order it is a breach of justice to take our own lives, the lives of which we are stewards. Suicide is, to put it plainly, an unjust act—unjust to God who gave us life; unjust to loved ones, who suffer so much anguish; and unjust to the wider community, whose human bonds are weakened by the act of suicide. It does no one any good to pretend otherwise. Thus the *Catechism* continues, suicide "offends love of neighbor because it unjustly breaks the ties of solidarity with family, nation, and other human societies to which we continue to have obligations. Suicide is contrary to love for the living God" (*CCC*, 2281).

MORAL CULPABILITY AND PSYCHOLOGICAL FACTORS

That is not the full story, though. If this remains the teaching of the Church after all, why the changes in liturgical and pastoral practice? Because while the teaching has not changed, circumstances surrounding the two prudential judgments have changed considerably. Let us return to the two reasons for the Church's former practice of denying funeral and burial to those who took their own lives. The first prudential judgment concerned the moral culpability of the person who dies by suicide. When someone takes his or her own life, loved ones almost immediately want to know why—to understand the reasons for such an act. Like all human behavior, and perhaps nowhere more than in suicide, motivations can be complex. Part of the pain of coping with it is precisely the fact that the reasons can seem so inscrutable. Today, though, there is a keener awareness of the complexity of human behavior and psychology, especially when it comes to the drastic act of suicide, and this awareness calls for a more modest evaluation of culpability. The Church is therefore more cautious in determining guilt among those who take their own lives.

As the *Catechism* teaches, "grave psychological disturbances, anguish, or grave fear of hardship, suffering, or torture can diminish the responsibility of the one committing suicide" (*CCC*, 2282). Thus, while the nature of the act itself remains gravely wrong, the gravity of the decision may not be adequately known or deliberate and hence less blameworthy. The knowledge of the sin, or the freedom in choosing it, may well be diminished by psychological factors that we understand better today than in the past. These factors include the psychological repercussions of trauma, mental illness, severe addictions, and especially depression. These afflictions can fill one with internal anguish and dysphoria that cloud rational judgment, foster an intense feeling of desperation, and cause such tunnel vision that self-inflicted death, however irrational, seems to be the most rational choice. As a result, the *Catechism* concludes, "We should not despair of the eternal salvation of persons who have taken their own lives. By ways known to him alone, God can provide the opportunity for salutary repentance. The Church prays for persons who have taken their own lives" (*CCC*, 2283).

Since we are genuinely uncertain of a person's psychological state and moral freedom in the dreadful act of suicide, it is so important to pray earnestly for our loved ones who have died in this way. One of the most consoling aspects of Catholic teaching is the spiritual accompaniment that we can exercise with all the dead. They are no longer with us on earth, but our relationship with them has not ended. Those who are being purified and prepared for the banquet of heaven are in greater need of our prayers than ever. The Church therefore encourages us to pray for all the dead, especially those closest to our hearts. Families of those who have died by suicide, whose culpability may well have been diminished by psychological and emotional factors, have a special responsibility to pray for their loved ones. Indeed, the most powerful prayer we make as a Catholic people is in the Holy Mass, which we can offer frequently for our beloved dead and especially for those who have taken their own lives.

SECULARIZATION AND CHANGING PASTORAL PRACTICE

The second pastoral judgment of the Church regarding funerals and burials, the more decisive one historically, involved the potential for "scandal" or copycat suicides. This remains a very real concern, and it should be addressed at the level of the family, the school, and the community. At the same time, the Church has—rightly, I think—judged her own influence in this matter to have waned in the face of widespread secularization. To be frank, we do not live in an age where the threat of withholding a Church funeral and burial provides much of a deterrent, either to the person who is suicidal or potential copycats. Pastoral care of the family, and prayers for the deceased, are deemed the greater goods today, allowing the Church to offer all her fervent prayers and supplications on behalf of the souls of the deceased, even those who take their own lives.

This secularization of society offers an additional point for reflection on the Church's teaching regarding suicide. As Archbishop Salvatore J. Cordileone wrote in the previous chapter, St. Thérèse of Lisieux whispered to one of her Carmelite sisters during her final days, "If I had no faith, I would have inflicted death on myself without hesitating a moment." She struggled mightily in her short life with temptations against faith, temptations that she heroically resisted in spiritual atonement for the rampant growth of atheism in her day. Her honest warning of a worldview in which God is absent makes an important point for an age like ours, which has almost entirely drained supernatural truths from our everyday lives.

In the cultural air that we all breathe, the bracing reality of God—of God's sovereignty, of divine providence—is almost entirely bleached out. When there is no cultural reinforcement of our belief in a Creator, in a loving Father, in spiritually meaningful suffering, then the flight into suicide becomes more plausible, attractive—even falsely considered "courageous" by some—and hence more understandable. Perhaps the greater latitude given by the Church these days to those who tragically end their own lives is a recognition that the cultural state of the world is not as conducive to faith and a supernatural outlook as it once was. As a result, those who take their own lives may, in part, have been led down that dreadful road by flawed cultural assumptions that we all have a duty to try to correct.

GOD'S MERCY AND THE HOPE OF ETERNAL LIFE

The Church's teaching on suicide, while ancient and firm, can be difficult to receive, especially by those whose loved ones have taken their own lives. Our convictions of faith continue to guide our behavior on the path to everlasting life, and those convictions can never be set aside, even to ease our pain about the death of those we love. At the same time, the Gospel—the Good News—even when it is hard, is always *good*. After all, those convictions about suicide, about God's sovereignty, are accompanied by equally strong convictions that he is the most loving of Fathers, who sees into the secret depths of each of our hearts, knows our deepest motivations, and—in mysterious ways known to him alone—"can provide the opportunity for salutary repentance" (*CCC*, 2283) while he lovingly invites each of us to the banquet of eternal life.

KEY POINTS

- In the past, canon law denied Catholic burials to people who died by suicide, primarily because of the moral gravity of the act and in order to deter other suicides.
- The teaching of the Church on suicide has not changed: we are stewards, not owners, of the life God has entrusted to us. It is not ours to dispose of. It is a grave injustice against God and one's neighbor.
- The Church's pastoral practice, however, has changed due to a keener awareness of psychological and emotional factors that can diminish moral culpability. In addition, widespread secularization has weakened the deterrent effect of withholding funerals.
- The Church prays for those who have died by suicide. We should not despair of their eternal salvation.

ASK YOURSELF

1. Do I know people who have felt shame because their loved one died by suicide? How can I share Church teachings in such a way as to bring comfort to those who grieve because of a suicide?
2. Can I explain why canon law previously denied funerals and burials to people who died by suicide? Do I have clear in my mind what cultural and theological shifts led to changes in pastoral and liturgical practice when someone dies by suicide?
3. How can the Church's teachings, prayers, and practices around suicide promote a culture of life?

9.

Discussing the Hard Questions and Accompanying the Grieving

Bishop John Dolan and Deacon Ed Shoener

Priests, deacons, and laypersons in grief ministry are sometimes called to accompany survivors of suicide loss. We are called upon to bring the Light of Christ into their darkness and help guide them to a hope that can only be found in his Resurrection. Our own faith may be challenged by the awful circumstances of suicide and the hard questions some survivors ask of us:

- How will my loved one be judged by God?
- Is my loved one in hell?
- Will they be punished in purgatory?
- Is it possible for my loved one to go to heaven?
- Can I pray for my loved one who died by suicide?
- Can my loved one who died by suicide pray for me?

These questions may never actually be spoken in your presence. It may be that a survivor is simply looking for support and consolation—the most basic pastoral care—which the Church has come to call "accompaniment." Many survivors will simply want a representative of the Church to be there. However, should these questions be asked, it is important to remember some key teachings of the Church on death, judgment, purgatory, heaven, and hell.

Addressing these teachings in times of grief requires humility and compassion on the part of the minister. We stand on holy and sacred ground as we see the suffering Christ in the grieving person who stands before us. We cannot make their pain, grief, and suffering go away. That is not within our power. But the Holy Spirit will work through us as we pour the healing balm of Christ's love upon the wounds of survivors of suicide. This spiritual balm is contained, in part, within the teachings of Christ's Church. Christ's mercy flows through these teachings. Coupled with charity, these teachings offer hope in a compassionate Christ who calls us to himself.

We know these teachings will be important, but we should always lift our hearts to God before and during any conversation with a person grieving a suicide. The person before us is deeply wounded. Christ is the divine physician. We are not. Yet we are privileged as God's ministers to be in conversation with the grief stricken. Therefore we should always remember to invite God into our hearts as we let the Holy Spirit guide our conversations.

ESCHATOLOGY: A REVIEW OF THE FOUR LAST THINGS

Our faith tradition considers four last things (eschatology) when we close our eyes on this life: death, judgment, heaven, and hell. According to our *Catechism*, "Each man receives his eternal retribution in his immortal soul at the very moment of his death, in a particular judgment that refers his life to Christ: either entrance into the blessedness of heaven—through a purification or immediately—or immediate and everlasting damnation" (*CCC*, 1022).

Regarding purification, the Church's teaching on purgatory in the *Catechism* is short and direct: "All who die in God's grace and friendship, but still imperfectly purified, are indeed assured of their eternal salvation; but after death they undergo purification, so as to achieve the holiness necessary to enter the joy of heaven" (*CCC*, 1030).

PRAYING FOR ALL SOULS

Although the Church does not teach that there is universal salvation, the Church expects the faithful to pray as if all can be saved. The Fatima prayer for Jesus to "lead all souls into heaven, especially those in most need of thy mercy" and St.

Faustina's Divine Mercy request that Jesus atone for "our sins and those of the whole world" are just a couple examples of our response to the Lord who himself prayed "may all be one" (Jn 17:21).

When a loved one dies by suicide, many wonder how they can show the one who has died that they are still loved. The simple answer is that we pray for them. As we celebrate a Mass or obtain indulgences on their behalf "through works of devotion, penance and charity" (*CCC*, 1471–1478), we offer up the pain of our suffering for those who have gone before us (*CCC*, 1032).

The Church's teaching on purgatory is beautiful and can be a source of comfort for survivors as we pray together for those who have died by suicide. Reciting the following prayer offered at funerals is healing for both the deceased and their survivors:

> Eternal Rest grant unto them, O Lord,
> and let perpetual light shine upon them.
> May they rest in peace. Amen.
> May their soul and the souls of all the faithful departed through the mercy of God, rest in peace. Amen.

In turn, we trust that those who have gone before us, including those who are experiencing the purification of purgatory, continue to pray for us. Those in the state of purification are in communion with us who live in this world *and* with those who enjoy eternal beatitude in the fullness of heaven. *Lumen Gentium* expresses this perfectly:

> Until the Lord shall come in His majesty, and all the angels with Him and death being destroyed, all things are subject to Him, some of His disciples are exiles on earth, some having died are purified, and others are in glory beholding "clearly God Himself triune and one, as He is"; but all in various ways and degrees are in communion in the same charity of God and neighbor and all sing the same hymn of glory to our God. (*Lumen Gentium*, 49)

JUDGMENT

The nature of purgatory, heaven, and hell are not nearly as important for us as the questions of how we will be judged and who will do the judging. As Catholics, the answer is simple. All of humanity will, in a particular and then a universal way, stand before the judgment seat of Jesus Christ, who is our judge. Matthew chapter 25 gives us a glimpse of the judge who will separate us, as a shepherd separates sheep from goats.

If we live and die faithfully and lovingly in Christ, we have a moral assurance that we will be judged mercifully and that heaven will be our reward. If we refuse to live faithfully and lovingly in Christ, scripture refers to those who will be judged harshly and will be found in hell. There is simply death, judgment, hell, or purgatory and heaven.

What is not found in the *Catechism*, sacred scripture, or the tradition of the Church is permission for us to usurp the role of Christ Jesus and become the judge of the dead. This belongs to Christ and the mercy of God alone. Mercy is generously poured out upon all of humanity because we are a sinful people. We are a people who live in a realm of concupiscence and, being forever tempted, we are apt to sin.

Our faith teaches that from the moment sin entered the world, God began a plan of redemption as proclaimed in the Exsultet of the Easter Vigil, each year.

> O truly necessary sin of Adam,
> destroyed completely by the Death of Christ!
> O happy fault
> that earned so great, so glorious a Redeemer!

Covenant after covenant, from Adam through Noah, Abraham, Moses, King David, the Prophets, and to and through Christ Jesus, God revealed his mercy. Gratefully, God's mercy is unmerited.

Scattered through the pages of history, human beings showed glimpses of true virtue and fidelity. Of course, the same pages show a human world of vice and downright evil. We are physical beings with souls of intellect and free will who were made in the image and likeness of God. This is a starting point for understanding our uniqueness in all of God's visible and invisible creation. Yet we are tempted and inclined to sin (concupiscence); we willfully succumb to sin and veer away from the will of God. Our conscience, on the other hand, urges us to remain with God and to live virtuous lives. On a very basic level, this "doctrine of humanity" is the Church's teaching of our human condition.

However, a development of the doctrine on the dignity of the human person acknowledges concupiscence as something more than just a rational or willful choosing of vice versus virtue. An understanding of the doctrine of the human person must recall this reality that the sciences of psychology and psychiatry continue to provide. Whether through chemical, biological, or situational realities (post-trauma, childhood abuse, drug-dependent homes, etc.), many of us do not, in fact, freely and willfully choose to abandon God or human virtues. Due to these situations, there is some lack of culpability or blameworthiness. In the case of those who have died by suicide, this understanding of our human nature must always be considered.

A COMPASSIONATE PASTORAL RESPONSE TO SUICIDE

In 2018, the bishops of California issued a pastoral letter titled "Hope and Healing"[1] on caring for those who suffer from mental illness. The letter took an in-depth look at the spiritual and pastoral issues surrounding mental illness as well as suicide. The letter was widely praised and described as "the new standard for mental health ministries around the world."[2]

In their pastoral letter, the bishops addressed the issue of suicide, which is all too often associated with mental illness. The letter provides authoritative pastoral guidance to Catholic leaders on the attitude that ministers should have when they minister to people who are grieving a suicide. The bishops addressed "the heartbreaking tragedy of suicide" and said that "those who have lost loved ones to suicide . . . suffer especially painful wounds and are particularly in need of our compassion and support." They wrote,

> Those who lose a loved one to suicide need particular care and attention, often for considerable periods of time. They have not only lost someone dear to them and are deeply grieving, their intense grief is often complicated by feelings of shame, confusion, anger or guilt. They may replay in their minds their last conversation with the loved one and wonder whether they could have done more to prevent the tragic death. Furthermore, they often feel alone and misunderstood, as though they cannot discuss this with anyone. Catholics must convey to them that we are not afraid to open this difficult conversation, that they need not feel ashamed to discuss their profound anguish and loss. While healing in these situations happens only very slowly, we must be willing to walk this long road with suicide survivors, to help console them with our unconditional friendship and with sensitive pastoral care.
>
> Let us remember that Christ's heart—a heart both human and divine—is merciful beyond measure. It is here that we place our hope. It is into Christ's hands stretched out on the cross that we entrust our loved ones who are suffering and all who have died as a result of a mental illness. We pray that the departed may find God's peace, a peace that surpasses all understanding. We pray that the angels will one day welcome them to that place where their grief will be extinguished, where they will suffer no more.

AVOIDING THREE FORMS OF JUDGMENT

If, as the California bishops proclaimed, God's mercy is "beyond measure," then we must approach suicide with mercy as well. As ministers, we should avoid three things when addressing suicide—namely, a tendency to be overly judgmental, overly psychoanalytical, and overly spiritual.

A real-life example of a priest who accused parents of aiding in their son's suicide because they had not brought him to weekly Mass points to a serious lack of charity and bad judgment. Another case involved a deacon who asked a grieving family if he could find a priest to offer an exorcism for their son's bedroom—this is an example of judging through over-spiritualizing the suicide.

Suicide is a very complex matter, and a simple answer as to why a person would take their own life is often a mystery that cannot be explained by faith or reason. Nevertheless, priests and ministers tend to weigh in on the matter and try to provide answers. More often than not, it is simply best to listen to and prayerfully support those who are grieving a suicide and not attempt to offer reasons for the tragedy.

As we consider the act of suicide, we must be reminded that that one act cannot define the level of fidelity that the person who died by suicide had in his or her life. There are many charitable, loving, and faithful souls who are also lost in a world of psychological oppression. It is our prayer that God does not judge us by a singular act but rather on our general and fundamental stance in life.

Whether or not the person who jumps from a bridge cries out at the last moment to God for mercy, God understands the nature of that person. It would be rare that a person who died by suicide did so by acting with his or her full use of intellect and free will. It is also an oversimplification to assume that a suicidal person has a lack of faith in God. As pointed out earlier, the development of the doctrine on the dignity of the human person allows the sciences of psychology and psychiatry to weigh in on each person's level of culpability, even while that person seeks a right relationship with our loving God.

This isn't to say that we aren't called to be virtuous people. Christianity demands a carrying of the cross daily, an exercise of faith, and a life of charity. However, simply put, some people due to their psychological makeup, life circumstances, and other factors are more equipped to be virtuous than others.

Suicide is clearly different from death through natural or accidental causes. The Church will forever say it is never right to end one's own life. The act of suicide, in and of itself, is a grave matter. The act, however, is one thing; the intention and the circumstances that lead up to that act is another. When a person who has bipolar disorder, schizophrenia, or a posttraumatic disorder ends their own life, it is assumed that they were not of the right mind to willfully act against our common and basic human instinct to live. This does not dismiss the gravity of the act itself. In fact, it is sinful in that it "misses the mark" (a Greek expression for sin) of what it means to live and love happily with God, with others, and with oneself. But it certainly puts things into perspective if we are inclined to pass judgment on suicidal persons.

As discussed in other chapters in this book, suicide was once judged by many in the Church based purely on the act itself. For this reason, a person who died by suicide was not permitted a Christian burial. Today, Christian burial is not only encouraged but expected as the Church responds to suicide with a new level of compassion based on our understanding of the psychological complexities of the human mind.

AVOIDING PSYCHOANALYSIS AND TREATMENT

Often, when family members approach a parish for a funeral of a loved one who has died by suicide, the pastor or bereavement ministers will make an effort to offer additional support through one-on-one or grief support group sessions.

Invariably, sessions will include some conversations about the deceased's history of mental health. In some cases, it is revealed that there were no signs at all that the person was ever suicidal. Some pastors or bereavement ministers tend to try to answer the reason for suicide by psychoanalyzing the situation.

This too can be a form of judgment. Although it is not an attempt to judge the soul, it is an attempt to fix or clean up the mystery of death by suicide. Walking the family through the mystery of death as it relates to the mystery of the Cross is one important element of the pastoral care of the grieving. But it is not the place of a pastor or parish minister to delve into the fields of psychology and psychiatry and attempt to offer a postmortem psychological diagnosis to explain why a person died by suicide.

Parish ministers are meant to accompany individuals and their families who are grieving a suicide, not offer psychological counseling or therapy. Pope Francis often uses the word *accompaniment*. Accompaniment simply requires an atmosphere of prayer, presence, and peace. Accompaniment gives those who are grieving a suicide an avenue to talk about their feelings and emotions. Because of this, some knowledge of psychological dysfunction, addiction, and mental illness is crucial to becoming a loving support to those who grieve one who died by suicide.

Stepping beyond the zone of accompaniment and into the world of psychoanalysis and treatment not only puts the clergy member or Catholic mental health minister in a place of legal liability but also may hamper persons who are struggling with depression or complicated grief from seeking professional help. In fact, parishes should obtain a list of psychologists and grief counselors who have verified licenses to assist parishioners. These lists may be obtained from county social agencies or from a local Catholic Charities office.

AVOIDING OVER-SPIRITUALIZING

While some ministers psychoanalyze suicidal events, others tend to over-spiritualize suicide. The real-life case about the deacon who asked a family if they would like a priest to exorcise their home after the suicide of their loved one is an example of overspiritualizing an event.

Some priests and ministers seem to find the devil behind every corner and think that prayers of exorcism or deliverance will address the cause of strife in a person's life. When it comes to depression, suicide, or attending to survivors of suicide loss, such over-spiritualization is not helpful and may actually be harmful.

Similar to psychoanalyzing the cause of suicide, over-spiritualizing the event—for example, suggesting that "the devil made them do it"—is a form of judgment. Again, it may not be judging the person per se, but attempting to solve the mystery of suicide prematurely. It does a disservice to the field of psychology that, we are convinced, is Spirit driven.

FIND THE RIGHT BALANCE

Our Church recognizes and celebrates the two disciplines of faith and science as having the same end. Faith and science lead us to God. They go hand in hand, and they are perfectly balanced. As ministers, we are encouraged to keep them in balance when we offer spiritual support. To either psychoanalyze or over-spiritualize a suicidal event tilts the balance and may cause unnecessary suffering.

Offering prayerful support through accompaniment is the first step that should be adopted by Catholic leaders when addressing survivors of suicide loss or people who may be depressed. The second is to refer those affected by depression or complicated grief to mental health professionals. Having a list of professional counselors at hand is always helpful.

As priests and ministers, judging a suicidal person's soul or the act of suicide itself does not belong to us. Rather, we are asked to entrust to the Lord those who have died by suicide and ask the Merciful Judge to grant them eternal rest. As

Pope Francis once said about those who have died by suicide, "To the very end, to the very end, there is the mercy of God."[3]

In the end, we are called to be merciful as Christ is merciful, to entrust the souls of the faithful departed to God, and to accompany those who grieve, including survivors of suicide loss.

KEY POINTS

- To accompany a person who is grieving the death of a loved one by suicide requires you to be with them in the darkness of grief. You may be asked hard questions about "the four last things."
- Christ's mercy flows through the teachings of the Church. These teachings can heal those who are grieving a suicide with the promise of the Resurrection.
- Purification can be found in purgatory. Christ will offer his mercy to purify a person of all that led to their death by suicide. We need to pray for the souls in purgatory.
- Pope Francis said about those who have died by suicide, "To the very end, to the very end, there is the mercy of God."
- We must be willing to walk the long road to healing with suicide survivors, to help console them with our unconditional friendship and sensitive pastoral care.
- As ministers, we should avoid three things when addressing suicide—namely, a tendency to be overly judgmental, overly psychoanalytic, and overly spiritual. We must find the right balance.

ASK YOURSELF

1. How will I discuss the question "Is my loved one in hell?" with a person who is grieving a death by suicide?
2. How can I ensure that I am spiritually and emotionally prepared to accompany a person who is grieving a death by suicide?
3. How can I use the teaching on purgatory to help a person grieve a suicide? What spiritual practices might I suggest?
4. Beyond preparing for the funeral, what can my parish or community do to "walk the long road" with individuals and families who are grieving a suicide?

PART III.

MEDICAL SCIENCE

What Psychology Teaches Us

10.

Suicide Assessment, Treatment, and Prevention

David A. Jobes, PhD, ABPP, with Ed Shoener

Catholic clergy and pastoral leaders are in a unique position to help parishioners who are grieving a loved one who died by suicide. A Catholic leader will be better equipped to offer consolation to those who have lost a loved one to suicide if they have a basic understanding of the nature of suicide based on the most recent scientific studies.

In this chapter I will provide information from my specialized field of study, clinical suicidology, to help you obtain some insights into what can lead people to suicide and help clear up some common misconceptions. In order to better understand the nature of suicide for pastoral work, it will also be helpful to understand how suicidality is understood and optimally assessed and treated from a clinical standpoint and why some approaches seem to work better than others (although there is no treatment method that is totally effective in preventing suicide).

SUICIDOLOGY

Generally speaking, suicidology is the scientific study of suicidal behavior, the causes of suicide risk, and the prevention of suicide deaths. I have been a clinical suicidologist for more than thirty-five years, working in this field as a researcher, clinician, and policy advocate. I am the director of the Suicide Prevention Lab at the Catholic University of America, and the focus of my work is broadly centered on understanding suicide risk and preventing suicide as a leading cause of death. We specifically study suicide risk assessment and treatment across a range of clinical settings with different patient populations. There is no question that the topic at hand can be quite painful and sobering; nevertheless, steady progress is being made within my field of study that should give us all cause for hope.

SUICIDE PREVALENCE AND TRENDS IN THE UNITED STATES

Suicide is a worldwide public health challenge; no population, culture, faith tradition, or subgroup is immune to the scourge of suicide, which ranks among the most tragic of human events. Suicide is the tenth leading cause of death in the United States. A staggering 10.6 million American adults have serious suicidal thoughts each year, while 1.4 million will attempt to take their lives. More than 47,000 people, across all ages, died by suicide in 2017.[1]

The suicide rates in the United States have gone up and down over the decades. For example, in 1914, the rate was 16 per 100,000 people; the rate in 2017 was about the same. We had thought that we had turned a corner in the 1990s when rates started to decline and were as low as 10.5 in 1999.[2] But there has been a discouraging and gradual increase over the last twenty years, with rates rising back up to the range of 16. These data are worrisome, especially in regard to suicide rates for young children, teenagers, veterans, and active-duty armed services members. We had thought that the rates came down in the 1980s and 1990s because of our innovative suicide prevention work and research, but the data suggest we still face challenges with this public health problem.

No one really knows why the rates have gone back up to historically high averages. Anyone who purports to know why rates have been increasing is merely speculating. There are known associations throughout history with the economy and unemployment, but this association does not account for recent rates. There is a lot of speculation about the impact of social media and disconnection and loss of faith, but these arguments have not been proven. Bottom line: no one really knows why the suicide rates have crept back up, but they are obviously concerning.

SUICIDE RISK FACTORS

The assessment of suicide risk has historically emphasized suicide "risk factors," which are largely demographic, psychosocial, and mental health variables that are correlated with suicide ideation (i.e., thinking about, considering, or planning suicide), suicide attempts, and completed suicides. Interestingly, a recent analysis of fifty years of risk factor research[3] has shown that risk factors have little to virtually no utility for understanding *prospective* risk for suicidal behavior. The research data is thus not very helpful for predicting who is going to attempt or die by suicide. While we desperately want to predict who is going to make attempts and complete suicide, our "fortune-telling" ability is terrible.

A statistic that is noted frequently is that 90 percent of the people who die by suicide have some mental illness.[4] That number is based on psychological autopsy research—intensive studies performed after a person dies by suicide (based on records and extensive interviews with loved ones). It is fair to say that psychopathology is mostly present in people who die by suicide. But there are millions of people who have psychiatric diagnoses that do not die by suicide. So knowing that someone has a mental illness does not really predict much of anything because, fortunately, people live with mental disorders every day, all the time.

Some have theorized that suicide risk is rooted in a lack of faith. But our clinical research does not show that a lack of faith is a significant driver of suicidal ideation. Within our research, we ask people very specifically, "What makes you want to kill yourself?" And it is relatively rare that suicidal people will say "My lack of faith" or "God has abandoned me." It is not that it never happens, but it is not a common response within our suicidal samples. That said, occasionally we will hear that faith is a consideration in their suicide musings. But in marked contrast, we see responses to the question "What makes you want to kill yourself?" overwhelmingly focused on relationship conflicts, what people do vocationally, and how they feel about themselves. In other words, based on our clinical trials across patient populations, issues related to work and love tend to be what plagues most suicidal people.

NOT EVERYONE WHO DIES FROM SUICIDE IS DEPRESSED

Many assume suicide is all about depression, but, again, rigorous research has shown that is just not true. If today is an average day in America, about 129

Americans will die by suicide; of those, maybe 40 or 50 of them will be clinically depressed, and the rest may have schizophrenia, anxiety, or substance abuse issues, as well as be experiencing all kinds of other stressors.

Given this, a common misperception about suicide is that if you treat depression, you are going to reduce suicide risk. There are now multiple meta-analyses (which are studies of studies) that do show this common presumption to be untrue. Thus the idea that depression and suicide are synonymous is just not the case. There are millions of Americans who are depressed who have no suicidal thoughts whatsoever.

Some years ago, there was a billboard campaign using the slogan "Depression kills." While it was a provocative slogan, there are more than seventeen million Americans who meet criteria for depression and clearly it is not causing the vast majority to take their lives (by millions). Only a very tiny subgroup of them will potentially take their life or make attempts. As will be discussed in more detail in the sections about treatment methods, the best treatments for suicide risk focus on suicide ideation and behaviors, independent from psychiatric diagnosis.

THE NATURE OF PSYCHOLOGICAL PAIN

The nature of psychological pain at the heart of suicidal states is fundamentally different from physical pain. Dr. Edwin Shneidman, a psychologist at the University of California, Los Angeles, called it "psychache." He created a word for it to make sure that it was different from depression, anxiety, or existential angst. Psychache is an exquisite suffering of the mind that is so unbearable that, in the mind's eye of the suffering person, it can only be extinguished through death.

Dr. Shneidman wrote, "Psychache refers to the hurt, anguish, soreness, aching, psychological pain in the psyche, the mind. It is intrinsically psychological—the pain of excessively felt shame, or guilt, or humiliation, or whatever. When it occurs, its reality is introspectively undeniable. Suicide occurs when the psychache is deemed by that person to be unbearable. This means that suicide also has to do with different individual thresholds for enduring psychological pain."[5]

The *Catechism of the Catholic Church* lists "grave psychological disturbances, anguish, a great fear of hardship, suffering or torture" (*CCC*, 2282) as factors that can diminish the responsibility of a person who dies by suicide. All of these can manifest in a form of psychological pain. Most suicidal people feel tortured and oftentimes have little remission from their suffering. What ultimately compels someone to end their life is thus an unbearable degree of angst and intense and pervasive psychological suffering that is fundamentally linked to the idea that the *only* way to end this suffering is through suicide.

WHAT OUR CLINICAL RESEARCH SHOWS ABOUT SUICIDAL IDEATION

Why and how does suicide as *way of coping* move onto a person's psychological radar in the first place? How do people become so preoccupied, even consumed, with suicide that it may prove fatal? My research team at the Catholic University Suicide Prevention Lab endeavors to study and address these exact thorny questions. We fundamentally study suicidal ideation and how ideation evolves into a potentially lethal behavior. Needless to say, it is an elusive thing to study. Suicidality can be quite nuanced, and it varies widely from person to person struggling with thoughts of self-destruction.

For people who are first experiencing suicidal ideation, such thoughts may feel like a kind of psychological hot potato. They feel uncomfortable, and they want to get rid of these disturbing thoughts. In contrast, there are people who have been ideating for a long time for whom such thoughts have become a form of comfort, providing a form of reassurance—"At least I've got this that I can do if things get really bad." We are tirelessly researching the different ways that people ideate and how these ideations evolve over time, which is a remarkably understudied topic within a field that is understandably preoccupied with behaviors.

Another approach within contemporary suicide assessment research that may be more helpful centers on "warning signs" for suicide—variables that may be more proximate to nearer-term behavioral risk. Suicide warning signs tend to emphasize highly dysregulated states of extreme agitation, upset, clear access to lethal means, and concrete plans for lethal action.

Another novel construct developed in my lab at Catholic University is the notion of suicidal "drivers," which are idiosyncratic problems *identified by the patient* that compel them to consider suicide as a means to deal with their struggles in life (i.e., a kind of "personalized warning sign"). Examples of suicidal drivers might include a patient being left by her husband, a sudden loss of a highly valued job, overwhelming and intrusive symptoms of historic sexual trauma or abuse, or posttraumatic syndrome flashbacks and nightmares that torture a veteran of combat.

TREATMENT OF SUICIDE RISK

It surprises many that the most commonly used interventions and treatments for suicide risk have little to mixed empirical support. People commonly associate suicide with a diagnosis of a mental illness and assume that if you treat the disorder, you can reduce the symptom of suicide. This commonly held notion has virtually no empirical support. As noted earlier, psychological treatments that focus on preventing suicide—no matter the underlying diagnosis—are the most effective treatments for suicide risk as proven in randomized controlled trials (RCTs). The RCT data supporting the efficacy of medications for reducing suicide risk is limited or mixed at best.[6] RCTs randomize patients into two groups: one receives the treatment under study and the other receives a control-comparison treatment. The treatments are then compared. RCTs are the gold standard within treatment-oriented research for proving that a treatment works in a *causal* manner, whether that be a medication or a psychological intervention.

Medications Have Minimal Impact on Suicide Risk

A common belief among those who lose someone to suicide is "If they just stayed on their medicine they would not have died by suicide." Such sentiment may reflect wishful thinking, but research support tends to show a very limited impact of psychotropic medications. Medicine can be helpful in managing certain mental illnesses and help people live in recovery.

When people think of treatment interventions for a suicidal person, they often immediately think of medicine before anything else. Let me be clear: if a patient of mine needs medication to manage certain mental disorders, I will refer them for medication because it can be effective for certain symptoms of mood-spectrum disorders or for psychosis (in particular). To be sure, when medications work, they can be a godsend. But according to RCT-based research, medicines do not necessarily help suicidal people, and in certain cases, certain medicines can actually make things worse for a suicidal patient.

The most common type of medicines used with suicidal people are antidepressants, specifically serotonin selective reuptake inhibitors (SSRIs), which can help some people with their depressive symptoms. But these drugs can have the side effect of making certain people over-activated (never good when suicidal thoughts are on board). Another approach—the low-dose use of ketamine through intravenous infusion—is generating tremendous excitement in the field. But the positive results are somewhat mixed and often very short lived (a matter of days). There is only one medicine—clozapine—approved by the FDA for a suicide impact among psychotic patients (based on one unreplicated randomized controlled trial).

In my experience, the general assumptions that are made about the presumed effectiveness of psychotropic medications for suicide risk is deeply rooted in a pervasive "medical model" approach to care, in which suicidal ideation is seen as a symptom of a mental disorder (e.g., depression, bipolar disorder, or psychotic disorder). The logic of the medical model is that treating the mental health disorder will reduce the symptoms of suicidal ideation and behavior. However, when we examine rigorous clinical trial research and meta-analyses, the evidence (with limited exceptions) overwhelmingly supports the direct and targeted treatment of suicidal ideation and behaviors, *independent* of psychiatric diagnoses.

This line of discussion does not argue that suicidal people should not take their prescribed medicines. But according to the existing research, these medicines are better suited to other psychiatric symptoms and do not yet show reliable impact on suicidal ideation and behaviors.

Hospitalization Is Not Necessarily Effective Either

Lengths of stays for inpatient care average about six days, and, to be candid, there is usually not much suicide-focused care during a typical hospital stay, as these brief stays tend to once again focus primarily on mental disorders and not so much on suicide risk and its proper treatment. The common presumption is that psychiatric hospitalization *must* be effective, but clear evidence for this assumption is lacking.

In my experience, people often go to the hospital thinking that, in a handful of days, something extraordinary is going to happen. The reality is that there is little "treatment" outside of starting medications and perhaps some group sessions prior to discharge. In a contemporary inpatient stay, the patient will have watched a lot of TV and gone to some groups until the utilization review staff come along and say, "Okay, get them out. They've been here five days." People are hospitalized so that they literally cannot kill themselves, yet every year there are about 1,500 suicides in inpatient psychiatric units. Perhaps more concerning are data showing evidence of *increased* suicide risk in the weeks to months following discharge.[7]

I began my career working primarily in inpatient psychiatric settings; I take no relish in being critical of the typical state of affairs. I still believe that in some cases, a well-timed hospitalization can be valuable and even life-saving. But there is clear and replicated evidence of an *increased* risk for suicide following inpatient discharge. Clearly we need typical inpatient care to become much more suicide focused, with an eye to post-discharge risk in particular.

Psychological Treatments

In contrast to widely used yet unproven treatments, a handful of suicide-focused psychological treatments are very effective for decreasing suicidal ideation and attempt behaviors as proven through replicated RCTs. Each of these treatments pursues the issue of suicide "like a dog with a bone." These treatments therefore systematically endeavor to take suicide off the psychological table for those who are convinced that "suicide is the only way I can end my pain." What is interesting about these proven treatments is that they effectively teach the suicidal person to understand that they do not get suicidal "out of the blue," but rather there is a particular way or a pattern as to how they get into trouble. If the patient comes to learn about this pattern, they can then avert the eventual suicidal crisis by problem-solving differently, without relying on suicide as a way of coping.

Dialectical Behavior Therapy

Dialectical behavior therapy (DBT) is a labor-intensive group-oriented treatment that teaches skills. There are four components: (1) a group in which members learn about coping skills; (2) individual therapy that helps craft these skills; (3) phone coaching, where the therapist and the patient talk on the phone over the course of the week; and (4) a consultation team comprised of therapists who support and provide feedback to the therapists who are providing the treatment. DBT has by far the best empirical RCT support for reducing self-harm behaviors and suicide attempts.[8]

Cognitive Behavioral Therapy

Suicide-focused therapy focuses treatment on what is referred to as the "suicidal mode," which is the state of mind, emotions, and physiology where people are convinced "I need to kill myself." There are two forms of this kind of treatment that have been proven to be effective for reducing suicide attempts: (1) cognitive therapy for suicide prevention (CT-SP)[9] and (2) brief therapy (BT).[10]

Cognitive therapy specifically teaches the patient to learn about the suicide modal state and then what to do when they get in that state. When a patient finds themselves heading into a suicide modal, they learn to use their safety plan, which provides them with a series of techniques to help them calm down, or seek out others' help or support, or do different things to get through that suicidal dark moment. A particularly novel innovation within this approach is the use of a "hope box," which can be an application on their phone or a shoebox filled with mementos and items that remind them of things that make their life worth living (a kind of live-saving memory aid).

Crisis Response Planning

A crisis response plan (CRP)[11] is a variation of safety planning that is used within the BCBT intervention. Within this intervention, the patient uses an index card to write down their triggers, their different coping strategies, and certain key people to whom they can reach out. It lists resources such as the Suicide Prevention Hotline or Lifeline (1-800-273-TALK) or the Crisis Text Line (741-741), and how to reduce access to lethal means to kill yourself, such as removing firearms. If the patient gets into an acute suicidal state, they know to rely on these coping strategies as a predetermined "game plan," which is in place to deal with their suicidal crisis.

Collaborative Assessment and Management of Suicidality

Collaborative assessment and management of suicidality (CAMS)[12] is a therapeutic framework that emphasizes collaboration, empathy, honesty, and a suicide-focus care that assesses and treats patient-defined suicidal drivers. It was developed at our suicide laboratory at Catholic University and is the most effective proven treatment for rapidly reducing suicidal ideation supported by five published RCTs. CAMS uses a series of forms that assess and guide suicide-focused treatment planning. The clinician sits next to the patient and together they use these forms for a suicide-focused assessment that helps describe what the patient is going through and then works to develop a stabilization plan to improve the patient's coping skills and ideally keep the patient *out* of the hospital if possible.

Patients like CAMS because they feel as though the clinician is not judging them or telling them what is wrong with them; instead, the patient "unpacks" what they are experiencing together with the clinician. CAMS is not a psychotherapy; rather, it is a therapeutic framework within which the patient collaborates with the clinician to do all suicide-focused assessment and treatment planning. Importantly within CAMS treatment planning, the clinician asks the patient, "What makes you want to kill yourself?" And the patient says things such as, "The voices, I can't stand the voices anymore." Or they'll say, "I watched this movie and it triggered this thing where I remembered that my father abused me for ten years, and it's all coming rushing back, and I can't sleep." Patients identify these very specific kinds of suicidal drivers, which are then specifically targeted and treated over the course of CAMS-guided care.

An Example of Psychological Treatment—Keith's Story

The case example of "Keith" (to preserve confidentiality, his actual name is not used) helps demonstrate the effectiveness of the CAMS approach. In this particular case, it is important to note that the role of spiritual support from his pastor, working in conjunction with his therapist, was central to his recovery from serious and potentially lethal suicidal thoughts.

Keith is a thirty-two-year-old Iraq war veteran. There was a particularly intense firefight in a small village, where two young children were shot and killed in crossfire with the enemy. The incident was investigated by the US Army and Keith was found not to be culpable for these tragic deaths. He finished the tour without incident, but upon return to the US, he began to experience severe symptoms of posttraumatic stress disorder and clinical depression.

To deal with his various symptoms, Keith began to drink heavily, which became a source of fighting with his wife. His symptoms grew worse as he experienced flashbacks of the firefight, and he routinely saw the faces of the dead children in vivid nightmares. On a few occasions, in highly intoxicated states, Keith had put his handgun to his head and prayed to God for the strength to pull the trigger to end his abject misery.

For Keith, there are several notable risk factors that include being a white male veteran with diagnosed PTSD and major depression. Keith had other significant risk factors—warning signs of agitation, ready access to lethal means, his repeated rehearsal behavior of putting his gun to his head when intoxicated, and alcohol-induced dysregulation—that were particularly concerning.

As his drinking and marital distress grew worse, Keith was given an ultimatum by his wife to seek mental health care or she would leave him. With considerable reluctance, he went to an outpatient clinic at the VA hospital where he saw a psychologist familiar with using CAMS. In their initial session they developed a stabilization plan (a variation on the safety plan notion) that included removing his weapon from his home during the course of care and an agreed-upon effort to decrease his alcohol use and abuse. As part of the treatment plan, Keith identified two drivers for his suicidal struggle: (1) PTSD symptoms, and (2) his marital conflict. The clinician promptly engaged Keith in prolonged exposure treatment for PTSD and referred Keith and his wife to couples therapy with a clinical social worker.

A critical breakthrough occurred in the seventh session when Keith admitted his fear of going to hell for having killed the innocent children in the fateful firefight. While his symptoms of PTSD were decreasing with effective prolonged exposure, this emergent issue of "moral injury" suddenly appeared as a new driver that became central to Keith's struggle. Keith was a "fallen Catholic" since returning from Iraq. Given this consideration, the clinician sought a release to speak to Keith's pastor so that he might pursue spiritual direction with the pastor as a "treatment" for his moral injury. While Keith was wary of the Sacrament of Reconciliation, the spiritual direction helped him immensely by gaining perspective on what he had done, and he began attending Mass again with his wife (which improved their marital bond as well).

Under CAMS-guided care, Keith's suicidality was resolved in twelve sessions. He ultimately decided to stop drinking altogether and their marital relationship was markedly improved as their communication and bond was renewed within an effective course of couples therapy.

THE LIMITS OF CURRENT ASSESSMENT AND TREATMENT METHODS

Despite hard-earned progress, still far too many lives are touched by the tragedy of suicide. It is therefore important to know about the specialization of suicide "postvention"—for suicide-loss survivors. To this end, many resources for those who have lost someone dear to suicide are available—for example, through the American Association of Suicidology (www.suicidology.org), the American Foundation for Suicide Prevention (www.afsp.orgwww.afsp.org), and the Suicide Prevention Resource Center (www.sprc.org).

I have spent more than thirty-seven years working on suicide as a clinician and researcher. I am sorry to report that over the past several years we have endured several suicides across two of our randomized controlled trials of CAMS. We work so hard to save these lives, so it is particularly heartbreaking to lose these patient-participants. We coach clinicians in our trials to do the best possible life-saving care we know to do, and yet despite our data and considerable expertise, patients in our studies have still taken their lives. It is a bitter pill, but we must live and persevere knowing all we can do is all we can do. While we can do a lot, it does not mean our care is guaranteed to work.

Suicide-loss survivors are often loaded with guilt and wonder if they could have done something. I understand. I think about my faculty colleague years ago who was literally across the hall from me. I think about the day when he stopped by my office door and lingered after some small talk then I turned back to my computer. I regret not having talked to him that day, because a few days later he took his life. While I do not think I caused his suicide, given what happened, I really wished I had talked to him that day.

More recently, we had a child in our neighborhood take his life by jumping off an overpass onto a very busy highway. I know that his parents did everything they could do. He was hospitalized three times, and he took lots of different medications. And they knew me, we were family friends, and our older sons were friends. If only we had . . .

Such is the nature of suicidal loss—so many questions, so many missed opportunities, and so many regrets for things that might have been done *in hindsight*. Such musings can be quite painful, and obviously no amount of hindsight will ever bring back this precious person. Survivors are thus thrust into a club that no one wants to join as a suicide-loss survivor.

FINDING GOD'S GRACE AND HEALING

No family, faith, or demographic is immune to the impact of suicide. As Catholics, we may wonder how God can abide the loss of dearly held loved ones by their own hand. The unanswerable hows and whys of suicide invariably haunt anyone who loses someone dear to suicide. While we may never have answers to painful questions of suicide, that we must do all we can to reduce suicide-related suffering—in all its forms—is inescapably compelling.

I know a couple who lost their beloved daughter to suicide. As highly educated professionals and loving parents, they did everything they knew to do to save their daughter. Their daughter was repeatedly hospitalized and had many different medications through the years. Since their daughter's death, I've been journeying with them to figure out how they can use their financial resources to have the biggest impact to prevent more suicides. I have so much admiration for what they are trying to do. But every time we have one of these discussions, they lose their daughter once again. But they continue to endeavor to turn this private tragedy into something productive so that, if possible, other people do not have to go through their nightmare.

As a clinician, I always pose the following question to my patients who are grieving a death by suicide: "How can you honor this person's memory?" I tell them that the best thing they can do is honor their memory and live as they would have you live. And that, to me, is the best advice therapeutically I can give—to carry on as this person would want you to live. I also gently suggest that their loved one should be remembered by how they lived, not by how they died. I believe that there can be some grace within these therapeutic efforts. But after many years of working in this field, I have come to know that within the wake of a suicide loss there can be a unique form of healing and some unexpected gifts that can be meaningful and even profound but nevertheless never bring back their precious loved one.

KEY POINTS

- No one really knows why suicide rates have gone back up to historic averages. Anybody who says they know why rates have been increasing is merely speculating. Although 90 percent of the people who die by suicide typically have some diagnosis of mental illness, knowing that someone has a mental illness does not really predict much of anything because, fortunately, people live with mental disorders every day, all the time. While we naturally want to be able to predict who is going to make a suicide attempt or die by suicide, our "fortune-telling" ability—even among experts—is terrible.
- Suicide has to do with different individual thresholds for enduring psychological pain, and there are warning signs and suicide drivers that are unique to each person.
- Medicine can be helpful in managing certain mental illness and help people live in recovery, but the existing research finds that medicines are better suited to other psychiatric symptoms and do not yet show a reliable impact on suicidal ideation and behaviors.
- There is not much suicide-focused care during typical hospitalizations, and there is evidence of post-discharge risk of suicide. Inpatient care really needs to become more suicide focused, with particular attention paid to the post-discharge period.
- There are psychological treatments that are very effective for decreasing suicidal ideation and attempt behaviors and they all are suicide focused.
- Despite hard-earned progress, far too many lives are still touched by the tragedy of suicide. We can do a lot, but that does not guarantee that suicides will not occur.
- No family, faith, or demographic is immune to the impact of suicide.

ASK YOURSELF

1. What are some of the unhelpful stereotypes that I have heard about people who have died by suicide? How do I want to respond when I hear a person attempt to explain a death by suicide using these stereotypes?
2. How will I use the information in this chapter to console a person who comes to me and is blaming themselves for their loved one's death by suicide?

3. A parishioner who is grieving a loved one's suicide visits and says, "I miss them so much. I think I may do what they did so that I can be with them." How do I want to discuss this statement with them? What would I tell them about medical treatments and psychological therapies?

4. How would I want to help and guide a parishioner who is grieving a loved one's suicide to answer the question, "How can I honor this person's memory?"

11.

Suicide Grief, Support, and Healing

Dianna Gonzalez, PsyD, LMFT

Understanding grief, the process of grieving, and the basics of how to minister to a person who is grieving are essential for a Catholic parish leader. I have seen firsthand how God works through parish leaders to bring comfort and healing to people who are grieving. It is a great grace.

When people lose a loved one to suicide, not only do they experience the usual grief reactions but they also experience unique challenges associated with suicide. Suicide grief can be especially traumatic and painful. It can impact the person's ability to cope because of the effects of stigma around suicide.

A common concern I hear often from people who are grieving the loss of a loved one to suicide is "I feel like I'm going crazy." Grief is always painful and disorienting, and suicide loss tends to magnify and further complicate the various and intense emotions a grieving person often experiences in very a short amount of time. Understanding grief in general, and the unique aspects of suicide grief, will help Catholic pastoral leaders bring comfort, normalize the experience of those grieving a suicide, destigmatize their loved one's death, and support these people and families in their individual journeys toward healing.

In this chapter, I will review the essential stages of grief—likely a refresher for many of you—and then discuss some of the unique aspects of suicide grief. I will also share some insights into cultural barriers that can impact how people respond to their pain. I will discuss how men, women, adolescents, and children can grieve differently. Finally, I will describe some of the healing strategies that I have found to be helpful when working with those who grieve suicide loss.

WHAT IS GRIEF?

After the death of a loved one, an individual can experience different feelings and emotions that directly impact a person physically, socially, emotionally, and spiritually. The intensity of the grief a person experiences varies depending on the attachment the individual had with the person who died. Grief is a process that is not linear, predictable, or stable; it tends to be an emotional roller coaster marked by many ups and downs, and twists and turns. Many people feel as if they are upside down at times.

Everyone's grief symptoms will manifest differently. However, some common physical symptoms experienced early in grief are fatigue, loss of appetite, sleep issues, and even illness due to continuous stress. Emotionally, a person can experience bouts of sadness, loneliness, anger, shock, and confusion. The emotions a person experiences can be triggered by memories, sounds, smells, and events. It is normal to feel fine one moment, and the next minute be in tears and feel completely helpless. Over time, these feelings tend to decrease in frequency and intensity as the person learns how to manage these feelings daily and moves through their grief.

Socially, a person can spend more time alone or even feel as though he or she cannot relate to others. Or a grieving person can experience the other side of the spectrum, where they find it challenging to be alone. Having a secure social support system is essential for helping people through grief. Spiritually, people may feel mad that God allowed their loved one to die. While some people turn to God during their pain, others can find it difficult to pray, read their Bible, or attend church.

Symptoms of grief may include:

Physical Symptoms

crying
fatigue
headaches
loss of appetite
difficulty sleeping or sleeping too often
eating too little or too much
increased susceptibility to illness

Social Symptoms

feeling alone
wanting to isolate oneself
feeling detached from others
anger that others' lives are going okay
self-destructive behavior (e.g., substance use)
not wanting to be alone; feeling needy and clingy

Emotional Symptoms

worry, anxiety, panic
feeling distracted, preoccupied
anger
confusion, overwhelm
sadness, crying spells
depression
fluctuating emotions
sense of lack of control

Spiritual Symptoms

questioning faith
anger at God
seeking solace in God
looking for the meaning of life and suffering

THE JOURNEY OF GRIEF

The process of grief can be complicated and might be experienced for weeks, months, and even years. There are a variety of states or phases that a person can experience while grieving. Elisabeth Kübler-Ross was a pioneer who developed a conceptual framework of grief that made an enormous impact on the treatment of grief and our understanding of death and dying. Junietta Baker McCall developed the journey of grief from the underpinnings of the Kübler-Ross model and added two new phases of typical response that allow the individual to reorganize their new reality without their loved one, instead of feeling as though they need to "move on from their loss."[1]

It is very important to note that these so-called states or phases are not linear, and a person can cycle back and forth from one to another. Also, not everyone experiences all of them. But these phases of grief have proven to be enormously helpful in understanding grief and the common experiences that many people go through.

Phases of Grief

Shock and Numbness

"I can't believe it!" or "It can't be true." Shock and numbness are normal responses when people first hear about their loss. This initial reaction helps the person deal with the pain and shock temporarily.

Denial

"Why me? This can't be happening" is a typical response to a loss. It keeps people from feeling overwhelmed and can give the person time to process the loss.

Feelings

Different feelings—anger, sadness, fear, confusion, and regret—are experienced These feelings can linger or be experienced in a short amount of time.

Depression

"I feel sad, why bother with anything?"; "What's the point?"; "I miss my loved one, why go on?" After a loss, they may withdraw from family and friends. They may feel numb and/or like they can't focus. They may have difficulty getting out of bed and prefer to be by themselves rather than around people. Some people start to look inward and want to make changes in their lives.

Reorganization

The individual focuses on the changes and new realities that stem from their loss. Reorganization empowers individuals to make small and large changes for healing to continue. Reorganization allows for the individual to take action with the changes they'd like to implement, which enables the person to learn and grow.

Recovery

This phase allows the person to find new meaning and accept their new reality without their loved one. Recovery is not focused on "getting over the loss or moving on." It's simply nourishing existing relationships and finding a new or redirected purpose to one's life.

COMPLICATED GRIEF

Most people will experience normal grief and adjust to their new reality without the person who died. The intensity and frequency of the feelings of pain start to decrease gradually over time, and these individuals begin to reorganize their lives and accept the loss. However, for some people, grief can be debilitating, and these individuals may have a hard time dealing with their sadness or any other emotions that are associated with their loss. Their grief then becomes what is known as "complicated grief."

Individuals who experience complicated grief suffer from their symptoms longer and with increasing intensity instead of decreasing over time. Complicated grief is a prolonged reaction, which continues to distress the individual throughout their everyday activities. The individual may have trouble adjusting to their daily life without the person who died. The intensity of their pain does not decrease, and the individual does not experience relief with their symptoms.

Signs and symptoms of complicated grief include:

- fresh grief linked to an old loss
- focus on little else but the loved one's death
- difficulty accepting the death
- numbness or detachment
- feeling that life holds no meaning or purpose
- trouble carrying out regular routines
- isolation from others and withdrawal from social activities
- experiences of depression, deep sadness, guilt, or self-blame
- feeling preoccupied with the loved one or how they died
- intense sorrow and emotional pain, sometimes including bitterness or anger
- inability to enjoy good memories about the loved one
- blaming oneself for the death
- wishing to die to be with the loved one
- excessively avoiding reminders of the loss
- continuous yearning and longing for the deceased

- feeling alone, detached from others, or distrustful of others since the death
- feeling that life is meaningless or empty without the loved one
- loss of identity or purpose in life; feeling like part of themselves died with the loved one[2]

THE UNIQUENESS OF SUICIDE GRIEF

What makes suicide grief unique is the traumatic aftermath and the grief responses of recurrent images, questions, guilt and shame, a sense of rejection and abandonment, and stigma that is experienced shortly after death to suicide.[3] Losing a loved one to suicide can leave a person emotionally and physically exhausted. These emotions can be felt days, weeks, and months after the suicide. Nightmares, recurrent images, flashbacks, concentration difficulties, and loss of interest in usual activities could become exacerbated if the person witnessed or discovered the suicide.

Suicide survivors are at a higher risk of developing posttraumatic stress disorder (PTSD), major depression, general anxiety disorder, and their own suicidal ideations. Their grief can cross over to complicated grief due to the difficulty of dealing with the trauma.

Different questions may arise after death to suicide. People can become overwhelmed with trying to find out why the person took his or her life. The search for the reason why the person took his or her own life is one that may never be answered. It can lead family members to create different conclusions as to why the person took his or her life. Moreover, this can strain family relationships, and loved ones may blame themselves or others.

Guilt and Shame

Guilt and shame often come up while working with families who have lost a loved one to suicide. Guilt brings a person false accusation of their loved one's death. Family members will self-blame for the loss, and this can lead to conflict within the family. Researchers have found that the feelings of guilt and shame stem from family members feeling as though they failed to help or get their loved one help or that they failed to notice that the person needed help.[4]

Feelings of guilt and shame can be experienced from the very beginning of receiving the horrific news of a suicide. I had the great privilege of working with our local police department on responding to crisis. Part of what I did was assist families when they received notification that there had been a sudden death, such as a suicide then I assisted the family in notifying friends and other family members. I recall getting a phone call from the police department to assist with a family who was going to receive a suicide notification. As the mother received the horrific news that her son had died from a completed suicide, in the midst of her pain, shock, and numbness the mother immediately told me that she did not want me to disclose to family and friends that her son had taken his own life.

Processing the feelings of shame and guilt will help people effectively deal with emotions instead of turning to negative coping strategies, such as alcohol or drug abuse. It's essential to be able to identify why the person feels shame, guilt, or responsibility for their loved one's death in order to prevent relational issues that could arise in a marriage or family. Helping a grieving person to understand why he or she feels shame or guilt is also crucial in order to help that person understand that the suicide was not his or her fault and move through the grief process in a healthy way.

Rejection and Abandonment

Feelings of rejection and abandonment can arise in suicide survivors. Survivors question whether they did enough to keep their loved ones safe or from harming themselves. The survivor can feel anger because the family is left behind to deal with such terrible pain.[5]

Some grief-stricken marriages struggle because each parent is left with their individual pain. They may blame themselves or each other for their child's suicide. The sudden, usually violent death of a child by suicide not infrequently leads to separation or divorce because of the rejection felt by each parent.

Researchers have found that children who have lost a parent to suicide also experience a profound and lingering sense of abandonment because children rely on their parents for most of their essential needs.[6]

Stigma and Suicide

Suicide survivors have a difficult time talking about their loss to others because of the stigma around suicide and mental health illness. This could leave survivors feeling alone, isolated, and even abandoned. With survivors, there is a sense of loss not only of their loved one who died by suicide but also their friends, family, and community.

In my experience, it is difficult for family members to acknowledge that their loved one was struggling with a mental health disorder or addiction. Suicide (or its ideation) may be stigmatized as a sin or as a sign of cowardice. Moreover, mental health is rarely spoken about as a health concern, and this prevents individuals from seeking help. This becomes a barrier to the individual struggling with their grief because their grief can manifest itself in other ways if treatment is not an option.

This can have deadly consequences. I recall a woman who was attending one of my parish bereavement groups. Her brother had died by suicide, and she stated he struggled with what appeared to be a mental health illness, which was never officially diagnosed. He refused to seek help, even when family members urged him to seek help. Another parishioner attending the parish grief group shared that her husband, who struggled with what was believed to be severe depression and alcoholism for years, also never sought help and sadly ended his own life.

Catholicism has a history of responding harshly to death by suicide, which has undoubtedly contributed to the stigma. Although the Church's understanding of suicide has changed, along with its pastoral practice and liturgical norms, as you read about in part 2, lingering misinformation and fear of the past practices of the Church can persist in some places. This fear of the Church's lack of understanding and harsh judgment prevents some survivors from openly talking or seeking guidance from their clergy and other pastoral leaders. Many families keep the cause of death a secret, which leads to isolation and confusion and deepens the shame around suicide.

In addition to the discomfort that suicide survivors have with talking about the suicide of their loved one, friends and extended family members do not know what to say to suicide survivors. Often friends and family will stay away, or the family avoids talking about death. This adds to the stigma, which increases isolation.

Trauma and Suicide

Trauma can be defined as a response to a distressing or disturbing event that overwhelms the person's ability to cope, and it can produce mixed emotions.

Death by suicide often comes without warning and can be unexpected and shocking. Sometimes the death is violent, which can create traumatic aftermath for suicide survivors. Those who discover their loved one's body report having trouble getting the gruesome images out of their minds. They mentally replay over and over their loved one's final moments or the last time they saw or spoke to their loved one.

A wife who lost her husband to suicide shared that going to sleep at night was the most difficult for her because she often experienced flashbacks and nightmares of finding her husband. Because of fear, she avoided the section of her house where she discovered him. In these situations, the person can start to experience traumatic distress and begin to have nightmares, anxiety, flashbacks, or fear of falling asleep.

The despair of the trauma can lead to anxiety, preoccupation with the circumstances of the death, insomnia, isolation, and hyperarousal when they think about their loved one's death. These symptoms can lead to developing a psychological disorder such as PTSD, depression, anxiety, or substance abuse as those who are grieving try to cope with their trauma.

Physical Health Care after Suicide

Experiencing a loss such as suicide is a significant life transition, and a suicide-bereaved person needs to be encouraged to take care of their physical health. In the beginning stages of grief, a person's rhythms are disrupted. It is common to experience loss of appetite or overeating, sleeping problems, difficulty focusing, decreased interest with sexual activity, or irregular bowel function.

Exercise can help improve mood, reduce stress, improve sleep, and regulate appetite. Before starting an exercise activity, it is recommended that the bereaved person consults a doctor to ensure that they are physically healthy. Nutrition enhances our well-being. Eating regular balanced meals may also help regulate bowel function.

Sleep is an integral part of our psychological and physical health. After a loss to suicide, survivors can experience a change in their sleep pattern because of all the stressful discussion, planning, and trauma that is experienced. These stressful activities can cause the body to produce an increase of the stress hormone cortisol, which increases alertness.

Tips for creating sleep hygiene:

- Go to sleep and wake up at a regular time.
- Avoid caffeine, alcohol, nicotine, or any stimulants before bed.
- Ensure your bedroom is comfortable and at the right temperature.
- Use bed only to sleep. Do not stay in bed if you are not sleepy.
- Avoid naps during the day.
- Create a sleep ritual such as lighting candles for meditation, a warm bath or shower, or prayer.

Culture Barriers and Suicide Grief

I have had the opportunity to work within a variety of cultures when counseling those who have lost a family member to suicide. Culture, religion, and language play an essential part in how people think, act, and speak about suicide. It is necessary to recognize how a person's culture understands grief and suicide. Different cultures may express grief differently. Some cultures tend to be more reserved than others. Openly grieving and expressing emotion can be discouraged in some cultures. Having an awareness of various cultural grieving practices and biases allows a pastoral leader to guide someone without prejudice as much as possible and to encourage that person to feel comfortable sharing their grief experience with a parish leader.

How an individual interprets their suicide grief and whom they ask for help are influenced by what was learned growing up. Often, cultural constructs become a barrier to seeking treatment for grief after a suicide because the person feels shame, embarrassment, and guilt and believes that they are going against the values of their culture. As a result, they are at a higher risk of experiencing complicated grief.

Every Family Is Different

Family influences how a person responds to their grief after a loss to suicide. Many of our beliefs, values, and behaviors are taught to us by our families, including systems of grieving. Consequently, the grieving person relies on what was learned in his or her family of origin to help cope with their loss. These beliefs, convictions, and behaviors will need to be attended to when you talk with survivors. Therefore, knowing the values and the family dynamics of how the family grieves is beneficial to understanding how the person expresses their grief. It also helps all those who are grieving understand the patterns of thought and behavior around grief that get passed down from one generation to another. As a pastoral leader and one asked to counsel those who grieve suicide loss, you may need to help navigate tensions and guide families especially to new patterns of responding to the many emotions they will be experiencing.

MEN, WOMEN, ADOLESCENTS, AND CHILDREN GRIEVE DIFFERENTLY

Grief is unique, but it is also helpful to understand some broad general tendencies among various age groups when we examine how individuals respond to their pain after suicide loss.

Men and Women

Men and women often have different ways of dealing with their grief. Women tend to believe that they are free to feel and talk about their emotions. Men, on the other hand, may have difficulty expressing their feelings or even allowing themselves to truly feel emotions, especially more painful ones. This gender difference can be made more intense by cultural norms. For example, in Latino culture, a common understanding of a certain machismo or maleness will keep many men from sharing emotions.

Men tend to deal with their pain alone, and they may feel that they need to fix it; they may be more solution-focused rather than accepting of their grief. Men are more likely to keep physically active and find solutions that can help solve their current problems, such as staying busy and trying to take their minds off their grief.

Women, on the other hand, tend to be more responsive to their emotions and often deal with grief and pain by expressing themselves. Many women are accustomed to talking about and processing their pain with others, whereas men frequently face emotions as something to be fixed.

Adolescents

Adolescents are in a phase of their lives where school is an integral part of their identity and peer relationships are the core of their everyday lives. Therefore, returning to school after they had a loss to suicide could be difficult because they may not know how to interact with their peers regarding their loss. Adolescents will often mask their emotions because they may not know how to express how they feel or they may feel that others are judging them. It is helpful to acknowledge and normalize the different emotions they may feel and encourage them to express their feelings. Some adolescents with whom I have worked had a parent, sibling, or friend die from suicide and showed a propensity to minimize the impact of that death.

As with adults, common feelings adolescents experience with a loss to suicide are anger, sadness, confusion, fear, and guilt. They can have difficulty regulating their emotions because often they can't understand what is happening and because the part of the brain that is responsible for regulating their emotions (frontal cortex) isn't fully developed. Adolescents can experience sleep disturbances, such as insomnia or difficulty maintaining sleep.

Adolescents may have difficulty expressing their feelings, especially if the expression of emotions is not something that their culture or family system embrace or if they feel that their peers are judging them. Adolescents can have difficulty focusing and concentrating in school after a loss from suicide, and it is common to see changes with their school performance.

Some adolescents can be consumed with their family's safety and well-being, trying to bring joy to the family, or taking over the role of the person who died in the family.

Young Children

Young children will grieve differently from adolescents and adults. Like adults and teens, the grief process will be unique to each child. Young children may have a lot of questions about death. Because some children may not understand the concept of death, they may wonder when their family member or friend is coming back.

Children sometimes act out and may engage in behavior such as tantrums, aggression, or withdrawal. Young children can also exhibit clingy behavior or develop separation anxiety from their parents. They may experience nightmares or sleep disruptions. Young children can also experience loss of appetite, irritability, or difficulty concentrating at school.[7]

SOCIAL SUPPORT FOR PEOPLE GRIEVING A SUICIDE

After an unexpected or traumatic death of a loved one, the survivors are left to deal with their grief. However, when the person who dies was well known to their community, communal grieving can offer extra support. Community support brings comfort to those experiencing loss. Showing support as a community can bring a level of healing and comfort for everyone. Different ways that a community grieves together are by having prayer vigils, hosting candlelight vigils, and creating memorials. The communal mourning allows everyone to support one another and provide support to the grieving family.

Support after a loss by suicide is essential. Social support is incredibly important for a person to receive after any kind of death, particularly with suicide. Unfortunately, oftentimes people will receive less support because of the stigma that is attached to suicide. Relationships can also be affected by the loss by suicide. Marriages can struggle, we can lose friendships, and it can leave a person or family feeling isolated or alone with their pain.

Many people are uncomfortable with accepting the loss and working through their grief. I often hear "I just want to feel better; to get back to feeling normal." I found that it's helpful for the bereaved person to know there is a space for them to share and express their feelings. Parish leaders can provide a welcoming space for the survivor to talk about the loss. Offering support, encouragement, spirituality, and hope can help decrease the negative stigma that may exist about faith and suicide. Helping survivors feel reconnected to their faith offers hope for many survivors.

Each person is going to have a different grieving process, and that is okay. As previously discussed, after a loss by suicide, a person can experience an intense mix of emotions. Normalizing and helping the person identify these intense emotions and reactions can help bring peace and movement toward healing.

PARISH GRIEF SUPPORT GROUPS

Sharing one's story and grief is beneficial to the healing journey. Grief groups bring hope to individuals by hearing other people's stories and learning to tell their own. Groups also allow the person to express his or her feelings in a safe environment, free from guilt, shame, or judgment. Sharing in groups also normalizes and validates what the individual is going through as a normal process, given their circumstances.

Parish grief support groups can be particularly helpful when relatives and friends may not be able to offer the support the bereaved person needs because of the stigma of suicide, cultural barriers, or lack of common faith convictions and practices. The support, love, and commitment expressed through well-directed parish support groups can be an indispensable part of healing for many Catholics who have experienced loss of a loved one to suicide.

PROFESSIONAL THERAPY

Catholic leaders must pay attention to expressed feelings, behaviors, moods, and thought processes of those who are grieving. These can be red flags that an individual ought to seek help from a mental health professional, such as a therapist, psychologist, or psychiatrist. If symptoms such as depression and exacerbated anxiety are impacting the individual's daily functioning, it can be a sign that the individual needs additional support. Warning signs include any symptoms of grief or complicated grief (see pages 98–102) that are becoming more intense over time. If depressive or anxiety symptoms become worse over time, instead of diminishing, then professional psychological or psychiatric counseling may be needed. Untreated symptoms can lead to complicated grief and depression, which can cause significant emotional damage.

Individual therapy can help grieving people process their feelings, develop new skills needed to overcome such devastating loss, and learn to manage their grief. It can alleviate symptoms of trauma and prevent complicated grief by helping a person talk about death and develop coping skills that can bring relief to him or her and help overcome feelings of guilt.

For couples, the death of a child can strain a marriage. Family therapy can help the couple address how each parent is grieving differently but also provide support for how the couple can grieve together.

Children often mirror the parents' grieving style. If an adult hides his or her grief, the child will more likely suppress his or her feelings. For a child, their life that was predictable has become uncertain and can become flooded with fear. Therapy can help children identify their feelings and can help process those feelings associated with death. Demonstrations of love and ongoing support are the greatest gifts a parent can give their child. If the parent is also grieving, make sure that the parent has enough support to work with their own grief while also supporting their grieving child.

HOLIDAYS AND SPECIAL OCCASIONS

Dealing with special occasions such as holidays, anniversaries, and birthdays can bring a wave of different emotions. It can trigger the person or family and make them feel as though they are experiencing a setback on the grieving journey. However, it is typical for grieving people or families to feel a little anxious, sad, or angry around special occasions that may bring up vivid memories of the loved ones they have lost.

What I found to be helpful is to talk about how the family can honor and remember their loved one's life and not focus on how the person died. Addressing the anxiety can be relieving to family members because they can see that their feelings are similar to those of others. Here are some ideas that clients of mine have tried:

- Make a special dinner or dessert that their loved one enjoyed.
- Celebrate the loved one's birthday.
- Light a candle and read a poem.
- Share stories of the person.
- Create a special ornament.
- Write a letter and perhaps read the letter to someone.
- Plant a tree.

- Say a special prayer.
- Create new traditions.

TAKE TIME WITH A PERSON'S HEALING JOURNEY

Remind the suicide-bereaved person that things will get better over time. This is difficult for someone to process, especially in the beginning stages of their grief, where the person can be flooded with shock, numbness, and disbelief. Providing hope, in the beginning, can give a person that little push they may need to begin to move forward. With support, compassion, understanding, and patience, healing will come.

KEY POINTS

- Grief is a process; it is not linear or stable; it tends to be an emotional roller coaster.
- Suicide grief has characteristics that are different than normal grief. These characteristics are quite often caused by stigma and the search for an answer to "Why?"
- People who are grieving a suicide often feel shame, rejection, and abandonment. Catholic leaders need to be aware of these feelings and make efforts to provide social support to people and families grieving a suicide.
- Cultures as well as family histories and dynamics influence how people grieve and particularly how people grieve a suicide.
- Grief after a suicide can turn to complicated grief, and help from a mental health professional may be needed.

ASK YOURSELF

1. When have I experienced the grief symptoms described in this chapter? How can I use my experience to help others?
2. What do I know of grieving rituals, attitudes, and traditions within the various cultural communities of my parish? How will I use my understanding in my care and outreach following a death by suicide?

3. How will I help a suicide-bereaved person overcome the shame, guilt, or stigma around suicide?

4. What grief support resources are in my parish and community to help a suicide-bereaved person or family?

12.

Posttraumatic Growth after Suicide

Melinda Moore, PhD
Department of Psychology
Eastern Kentucky University

All death unsettles us, but suicide leaves us with a very particular
series of emotional, moral, and religious scars.
It brings with it an ache, a chaos, a darkness, and a stigma
that has to be experienced to be believed.
Sometimes we deny it, but it's always there,
irrespective of our religious and moral beliefs.

—Fr. Ronald Rolheiser

Suicide, perhaps more than any other cause of death, challenges our ways of
thinking about the person who has died and our relationship to them. Inevitably,
existential and religious questions arise among the surviving loved ones, the suicide-loss survivors or "suicide bereaved," as they struggle with their relationship
to God and try to navigate this traumatic loss within the context of their practice
of faith.

Priests, deacons, women religious, and Catholic lay leaders who are ministering to the suicide bereaved are in a unique position to help navigate this very
isolating and confusing experience and, perhaps, bring comfort to great confusion. It is an essential Catholic belief that suffering can lead to spiritual growth
and renewal. In modern scientific parlance, this is called "posttraumatic growth."

THE IMPACT OF SUICIDE

Within the last twenty years, the science around why people become suicidal, how to intervene with a suicidal individual, and the serious and oftentimes deleterious health consequences of suicide on the suicide bereaved or on a community affected by a suicide death has evolved quickly. Nearly half of all individuals surveyed in several studies knew someone who died by suicide.[1] However, simply knowing someone who died by suicide does not necessarily signal significant emotional impact. Suicide impact may actually exist on a continuum (see figures 1 and 2), from suicide exposure to suicide bereaved, short and long term.[2]

The depth of impact is related to the suicide-bereaved person's perception of "emotional" closeness to the decedent—not necessarily biological connection or geographic closeness. This could be a college roommate, a neighbor, a work colleague, or a fellow parishioner. More problematic is the finding that suicide-bereaved individuals with higher feelings of closeness to the deceased are at elevated risk for serious mental health outcomes, such as depression and anxiety, as well as increased risk of suicidal ideation[3] and suicide attempt.[4]

The consequences are devastating for a community: for every person who dies by suicide, there are 135 individuals exposed to the death and about 30 percent, or 48 individuals, who feel "close" or "very close" to the decedent and potentially at risk for suicide themselves as a result.[5] Bereavement from suicide has been associated with psychiatric disorders such as prolonged grief disorder[6]

FIGURE 1

A NEW NOMENCLATURE FOR "SURVIVORS"

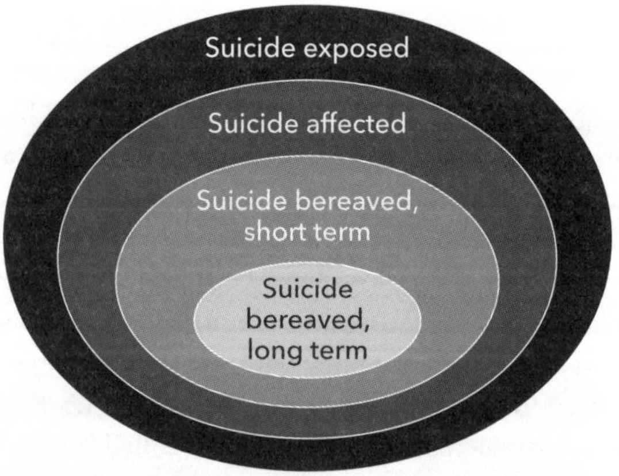

(Cerel, McIntosh, Neimeyer, Marshall & Maple, 2014)

and posttraumatic stress disorder.[7] Bereavement from suicide has been associated with psychiatric disorders such as prolonged grief disorder and posttraumatic stress disorder. More scientific inquiry is necessary to understand the mechanisms of the impact of suicide bereavement. Unfortunately, the limited research on suicide bereavement has focused on the psychopathology of this loss and the exposure to and impact of suicide may be so much more nuanced. For instance, there may be potential for growth in the aftermath of such an event.

Positive psychology, or the study of positive well-being, offers another vehicle for understanding the consequences of suicide loss by investigating the possibilities for personal growth or "posttraumatic growth" within the context of this distressing and traumatic event. Posttraumatic growth offers a new avenue for investigating traumatic events that acknowledges the unbelievable and shocking aftermath while also exploring the possibilities for positive changes that occur as a result.

If equipped with the right tools, faith leaders are positioned to help change the trajectory of the lives of the suicide bereaved and their grief journey in a profound and significant way. The work of the National Action Alliance for Suicide Prevention's Faith Communities Task Force—the nation's public-private partnership for suicide prevention in the United States—has been instrumental in attempting to inform and equip faith leaders with the tools needed to prevent suicide and provide care and comfort to those affected by suicide.

The 2019 resource *Suicide Prevention Competencies for Faith Leaders: Supporting Life Before, During, and After a Suicidal Crisis*,[8] developed in consultation with leaders from diverse faith communities and national suicide prevention experts,

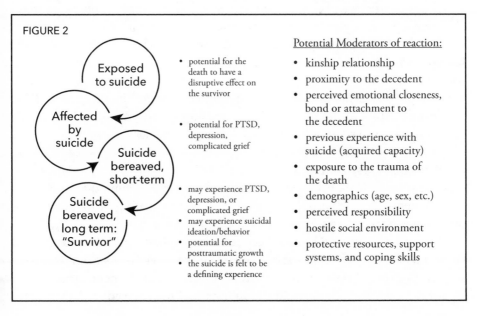

FIGURE 2

Exposed to suicide

Affected by suicide

Suicide bereaved, short-term

Suicide bereaved, long term: "Survivor"

- potential for the death to have a disruptive effect on the survivor

- potential for PTSD, depression, complicated grief

- may experience PTSD, depression, or complicated grief
- may experience suicidal ideation/behavior
- potential for posttraumatic growth
- the suicide is felt to be a defining experience

Potential Moderators of reaction:

- kinship relationship
- proximity to the decedent
- perceived emotional closeness, bond or attachment to the decedent
- previous experience with suicide (acquired capacity)
- exposure to the trauma of the death
- demographics (age, sex, etc.)
- perceived responsibility
- hostile social environment
- protective resources, support systems, and coping skills

presents feasible, practical, research-based actions that faith leaders can adopt immediately to help save lives and restore hope in faith communities nationwide. Postvention competencies (activities in the aftermath of a suicide) are included in the appendix of this book and are a start for faith leaders who are challenging themselves to become equipped to work with individuals who are struggling with suicide, their families, and the suicide bereaved in a meaningful way.

THE POTENTIAL FOR POSTTRAUMATIC GROWTH

> Even the helpless victim of a hopeless situation, facing a fate he cannot change, may rise above himself, may grow beyond himself, and by so doing change himself . . . turn a personal tragedy into a triumph.
>
> —Viktor Frankl, *Man's Search for Meaning*

Faith leaders have the potential to provide a sense of connection and belongingness for suicide-bereaved individuals of faith in the aftermath of their loss that allows them to survive this traumatic experience while profoundly growing in their faith and other dimensions. Posttraumatic growth (PTG) is an idea that has existed for thousands of years; it is reported in the Bible, in Greek and Roman literature, and even in Viktor Frankl's account of surviving a concentration camp during the Holocaust.

It was not characterized in the modern scientific era until the phrase *posttraumatic growth* was coined and an assessment tool for measuring it was developed in 2006. Dr. Lawrence Calhoun and Dr. Richard Tedeschi,[9] researchers from the University of North Carolina, pioneered the concept of PTG, characterized as a construct of positive psychological change occurring as the result of one's struggle with a highly challenging, stressful, and traumatic event. The presence of PTG can manifest itself in several ways, including an increased appreciation for life, better interpersonal relationships, changed priorities, an increased sense of personal strength, and spiritual growth.[10]

Posttraumatic growth has been investigated in a broad range of trauma survivors, including suicide-bereaved individuals. Research has found that suicide-bereaved parents demonstrated moderate levels of posttraumatic growth despite their profound experiences of grief and loss.[11]

Posttraumatic growth has also been found in studies of military veterans and family members of active-duty service members who died by suicide. PTG scores for suicide-exposed veterans and family members of service members indicated high moderate levels of growth in the aftermath of these tragedies. Additionally, elements of having greater personal strength and increased interpersonal growth show positive associations with PTSD, depression, anxiety, and prolonged grief.[12] Moreover, in another military-related study,[13] resilience and helping others accounted for a huge amount of difference in PTG scores among those who lost a close family member to suicide.

Knowing that growth after traumatic loss is possible provides hope to the individual who has experienced the loss, and also gives them tools for rebuilding their lives by giving them a real understanding of how they have been changed as a result of this trauma. Facilitating PTG is becoming an important therapeutic approach that both professionals and organizations serving those who have experienced traumatic loss may employ.[14] Faith leaders may foster this kind of growth in bereaved individuals and families, as it provides a perfect venue to learn how some families who have been through the worst are able to come out of this traumatic life experience in a way that their lives are forever changed, but they are more resilient and robust than they might have otherwise been.

What seems related to the likelihood of PTG is one's mental engagement with a traumatic event in its aftermath or one's ability to reflectively engage or "ruminate" over elements of the event in order to repair and restructure one's understanding of the world. Lowering anxiety and feeling connected and cared for may assist in one's ability to effectively ruminate on this event. This kind of rumination in the aftermath of a crisis leads to recognition that changes experienced are deeply profound and contribute to the building of a kind of wisdom.[15]

AN INSTILLATION OF HOPE

You can't live without hope. I knew that somehow, someway, I was going to have to rebuild hope. My son died by suicide. How could I rebuild hope in the face of losing him in that way? Surviving my son's death was barely survivable with my faith. . . . Without it, I can't imagine it being survivable.

—Kay Warren, cofounder, Saddleback Church
Plenary Keynote, Healing After Suicide Conference
American Association of Suicidology Conference
Washington, DC, April 19, 2018

Clergy and faith leaders are in a unique position to guide struggling souls when it comes to how we as the faithful think about suicide. The vocabulary used and treatment of individuals who may be significantly impacted or bereaved by suicide and at risk for suicide themselves can have tremendous influence. Faith leaders become trusted messengers of hope, assuring the bereaved that the sun will come up another day and that reconciliation is possible.

Each death presents challenges and opportunities, and no two suicide deaths are alike. One way of addressing the individuality of the deceased can be through "experimental restorying." This approach enables survivors of loss, through telling the story of the person's full life, to work through problems seen and unseen or even denied. This technique emerges from narrative therapy whereby an individual uses a story or multiple stories from their life to enrich their own life narrative, heightening emotional awareness and meaning.[16] The hearer gathers stories, analyzes them for key elements such as time, place, or plot, and collaboratively rewrites the story to place it in a sequence that makes sense for the person telling the story.

E. Betsy Ross related her own ambivalence as to whether or not to pray for her husband's soul after his suicide.[17] She turned to her minister, Pastor David, who provided comfort by reassuring her that she should pray for her husband's soul. He reminded her that the early Christians prayed for the souls of those departed Christians who had killed themselves to avoid Roman torture and assassination. It was only later that individuals who died by suicide were reviled and despised by the Church. By arming her with biblical wisdom and the authority of his position, Ross's minister helped shape the way she "restoried" her husband's death to confront and work through her loss, anguish, and shame.

Faith leaders are able to adopt this approach in working with stories of the Bible as they minister to the needs of the suicide bereaved. Using biblical or other religious stories as models of wrestling with faith struggles, the bereaved are able to openly process their questioning as well as their discomfort around questioning tenants of their faith.

Counseling by faith leaders in the aftermath of suicide may predict in part the trajectory of grief experienced by family and friends. Openly exhibiting your emotion, should the story touch you, should not be withheld. Listening carefully to their grief, confusion, and worry that their relationship with God has been inalterably disrupted because of this loss is essential. This latter concern may be a critical step in ministering to their spiritual needs, for many feel that they are wearing a "scarlet letter"—a mark of shame that everyone sees or knows about. The inability to integrate this loss into their understanding of a compassionate God or a sense of justice in the world is often an intellectual and spiritual disconnect that many suicide bereaved confront in their lonely walk into the unknown abyss of the future. Faith leaders can help them to find the rope bridge downstream that will carry them over this depth. For those who had no faith or relationship with God before, as a faith leader you can assist them through this minefield and perhaps help them in a spiritual quest.

MY PERSONAL STORY

After my husband's suicide, I recall sitting with a compassionate stranger, Fr. Bill Maroon, a priest to whom I had been referred by one of his parishioners in Columbus, Ohio. I was a new Catholic, having converted and entered the Church the year before my Conor's death. I was uncertain how to make sense of my new faith in the context of the most painful, most perplexing event of my life. "Why did this happen to me? Why did this happen to Conor?"—these were constant questions in my mind. Other clergy with whom I had come in contact had been unable to answer my questions as to how to assimilate this experience into my journey of faith.

Fr. Maroon sat and cried with me, recounting—really, reteaching in a profound way—the stories of Job's coping with enormous grief and his questions about where God was in the midst of suffering. "Where was God in this?"—in that moment of intense pain, I was given permission to question, like Job, God's whereabouts, to sink deeply into my disappointment and grief. Fr. Maroon gave me permission, not by telling me but by doing, by crying with me, by being present to my intense pain, and by restorying. Through Fr. Maroon's fearless compassion and restorying of Job, I was profoundly taught how close our modern-day experiences are to those in the Bible and how real God's mercy is for us and our loved ones. I will never forget this godly man and how healing his ministry of aftercare was for me. His care allowed me to begin the task of reshaping my grief.

Because Conor was Irish and came to the United States to study at the Ohio State University, I wanted to participate in an Irish tradition of the "Month's Mind Mass," a Mass that occurs one month after death as a way of celebrating the deceased's life of faith and commending them to the Lord. I thought this would be an opportunity to invite his friends and colleagues at Ohio State to participate in a memorial ceremony because they were unable to attend his funeral and burial in Ireland. I was in unchartered territory and was uncertain how the priest would handle the disposition of Conor's soul during the Mass. I was certain that his soul was with God, but my own friends' and family's reaction to his suicide, not to mention my community newspaper's and my work colleagues' apparent horror, communicated something different. Even a local priest, a friend of Conor's father, told me that he was not "certain of the disposition of Conor's soul," in response to my question about my own walk of faith. It was as if Conor's act of self-destruction clouded ministering to my own need for clarity about how to understand his death. I was certain that people who surrounded me weren't sure about his soul. I suspected they weren't certain about my soul either, and this made the experience of celebrating Conor's life of faith in a Catholic church—much less "commending him to the Lord"—uncomfortable.

I was also nervous because I knew the priests of St. Patrick's Church, a church supported by the Dominican order, were a more traditional, conservative order, especially Fr. Stephen Hayes, the American-born, Gaelic-speaking lawyer-priest who was going to preside at this Mass. I was nervous, but I tried to stay obedient in my heart, knowing that Fr. Hayes would handle it the appropriate way, even if it caused pain and discomfort in my own heart. When Fr. Hayes entered the church and began the service, he spoke with direction and clarity, asserting that Conor's soul was with God by virtue of his baptism. *He was with God.* All questions were vanquished, all doubt erased, and all misrepresented Church policy redirected. There seemed to be a sigh of relief among the attendees, as if they, too, feared condemnation. Fr. Hayes showed leadership, compassion, and a profound understanding in his very first utterance. I will never forget that moment and how it provided enormous comfort in my time of greatest pain, and buoyed my own faith practice, even all these years later.

KEY POINTS

- It is an essential Catholic belief that suffering can lead to spiritual growth and renewal.
- Faith leaders are in privileged positions to help provide a sense of connection and belongingness for suicide-bereaved individuals.
- Posttraumatic growth can lead to an increased appreciation for life, better interpersonal relationships, changed priorities, an increased sense of personal strength, and spiritual growth.
- Experimental restorying, perhaps by using stories from the Bible or the lives of the saints, enables survivors of loss, through telling the story of the person's full life, to work through problems seen and unseen or even denied.
- Openly exhibiting your emotion, should the story touch you, should not be withheld.

ASK YOURSELF

1. What stories from scripture or the lives of the saints come to mind that could help a person who is suicide bereaved?
2. What personal stories or memories about suicide am I ready to share with a person who is suicide bereaved?

3. Which of the pastoral postvention skills (activities in the aftermath of a suicide) listed in appendix 3 am I and/or our parish able to effectively implement?
4. Which of the pastoral postvention skills do I and/or our parish need to work on and be better prepared to act on when a suicide occurs?

PART IV.

CHURCH MINISTRIES

Offering
Hope and
Healing after
Suicide

13.

A Responsive Catholic Community Includes Mental Health Ministry

Wendell J. Callahan, PhD
Liberty Hebron, MA, LPCC
Alissa Willmerdinger, MA, LPCA
Catholic Institute for Mental Health Ministry
University of San Diego

A RATIONALE FOR CATHOLIC MENTAL HEALTH MINISTRY

St. John wrote of our Lord, "The thief comes only to steal and slaughter and destroy; I came so that they might have life and have it more abundantly" (Jn 10:10). For many Catholics suffering from mental illness, the stigma, shame, and, in some cases, shunning they experience create a barrier to engaging meaningfully in the life of the Church, moving closer to Christ, and indeed living life to the full. Our intention in this chapter is to provide a rationale for and describe the basic elements of Catholic mental health ministry. Our work is also guided by the simple and compelling principles outlined in *Hope and Healing: A Pastoral Letter from the Bishops of California on Caring for Those Who Suffer from Mental Illness.*[1]

Principle 1. *Christ calls us to attend to those who suffer from mental illness and provide hope and healing.* With this in mind, we believe that a basic understanding of mental health is imperative for all Catholic leaders, both clergy and lay ministers, participating in mental health ministry. Indeed, to minister effectively to those coping with mental health problems, a basic understanding of mental health, common terminology, and the process of initiate appropriate referrals is required.

Principle 2. *The scope and burden of mental illness in our society is enormous.* We are all affected by mental health concerns. Depression and anxiety are common to our emotional life as humans, and how we learn to cope and adapt to these experiences is often a lifelong process. Additionally, the impact of severe mental illness is often either felt directly in our lives or indirectly through the suffering and struggles of a loved one. Mental health problems are common, and effective treatments are available. An active mental health ministry equips the Church to help connect parishioners with appropriate referrals as well as to provide prayerful accompaniment as parishioners navigate treatment, crisis, and healing.

Principle 3. *Those suffering from mental illness should not be stigmatized or judged.* Mental illness remains poorly understood even by clergy and others in positions of influence. In the health-care community, mental illness is viewed as having clear neurobiological and genetic correlates, and treatment for most major psychiatric conditions involves both physical and psychological components. Mental illness should never be viewed as the consequence of character flaws or lack of faith. Imagine how ridiculous it would be to judge or stigmatize a parishioner with cancer or assume that a lack of faith caused their illness! Yet we continue to view mental illness as somehow different in its origin. As Catholics, we are called to reach out and embrace all of our brothers and sisters suffering from illnesses, and we need not treat mental illness as different from any other medical condition. Indeed, the Church recognizes St. Dymphna as patron of both mental *and* neurological disorders as well as mental health practitioners *and* neurologists.[2]

Principle 4. *The Church, health-care professionals, and scientific researchers should work together to improve mental health care.* An effective and sustainable response to mental illness in the Church requires a collaborative approach. We recognize that our work to promote mental health ministry necessitates that we engage meaningfully with clergy, laity, researchers, and practitioners to advance the notion and commitment to growing the ministry.

Principle 5. *We must meet and attend to those in need where they are.* Our sisters and brothers coping with mental illness are sitting next to us in the pews during Mass as well as sleeping in the Church parking lot at night. This means that we should design outreach efforts to engage known parishioners more deeply as well as connect our efforts to the community around us. How we organize our ministries will determine our degree of success in these efforts.

Principle 6. *Those impacted by suicide need our compassionate response.* Suicide is tragically a common symptom as well as a complication of mental illness. It needs to be understood as such, with no judgment. Instead, many loved ones of those who have died from suicide may live with shame or guilt. Therefore we must respond with embrace, compassion, love, and prayer. Our response as compassionate and prayerful companions can help to relieve this unnecessary pain and also make our parishes more welcoming and Spirit-filled communities.

MENTAL HEALTH CARE—AN UNMET NEED

The issue of mental health and the Catholic Church remains vexing primarily because many Catholic leaders and members of our clergy are not adequately prepared to respond to parishioners with mental health problems. This situation may be compounded by our tendency as Catholics, in comparison to other Christian groups, not to discuss mental health concerns with our clergy as described by Professor Christopher Ellison and his colleagues at the University of Texas.[3] The problem of mental health in Catholic parishes is one of high *unmet need* coupled with *low demand*.[4] That is, as Catholics, we are reticent to seek professional treatment and instead often sit in quiet desperation with untreated mental illness. This situation can interfere with our individual spiritual lives as well as hinder our coming together in communion as a parish community. The notion of unmet need is rooted in not only our tendencies as Catholics to not immediately recognize and seek treatment for mental health problems but also the fact that most Catholic parishes are poorly equipped to address mental health concerns. A parishioner's death by suicide brings this problem into sharp focus.

AN ALL TOO COMMON STORY— WELL-INTENTIONED BUT MISGUIDED RESPONSE TO SUICIDE

The case example below is a composite of actual events of which we are aware, but it does not represent any individual person's death by suicide. This example is here to illustrate what we see as the present state of mental health literacy and responsiveness in far too many US Catholic parishes.

Consider the recent case of Tim, a thirty-two-year-old single man, college educated and professionally employed, who died by suicide after struggling with severe depression since high school. Tim is from a devout Catholic family; his parents and siblings meet with their parish priest to arrange for the vigil prayer service and funeral Mass. The family members are distraught, and the priest shares his sincere condolences.

The priest proffers insights into Tim's struggle with depression as a consequence of lifestyle choices that diverted him away from God, and perhaps the struggle was even a form of "spiritual warfare" with Satan himself or one of his many demons. The priest goes on, with the best intentions, to state that "committing suicide" is often how someone chooses to resolve this type of existential/ spiritual crisis. The priest says that suicide is a sin, but the Church prays that God will be merciful to Tim.

The priest offers no additional resources or support to the family other than recommending scripture readings for the service. The remainder of the meeting proceeds in a businesslike manner and the family leaves to go home. At the funeral, the family is caught off guard and feels shamed when the priest says in the homily that, while we should pray for Tim, in order to prevent any more suicides he wants to make it clear that suicide is a sin and that he hopes no one else will *choose* to resolve their problems by *committing* suicide.

While Tim's case is certainly not how we envision our Church should respond to a death by suicide, it is nevertheless a common response. The pastoral response is well intentioned but not guided by current scientific and medical knowledge of mental illness. It has the potential to make the family feel disconnected or, in the worst case, ashamed about the death of a loved one. This stark reality of our Church's current state compels us to seek ways to become more responsive to suicide and ideally more proactive in supporting our brothers and sisters with mental illness.

MENTAL HEALTH LITERACY

The logical starting point for becoming more responsive to mental health problems, and certainly in the case of suicide, is to educate ourselves as Catholics about mental health and suicide. We call this "mental health literacy," and becoming knowledgeable (or literate) about mental health begins with understanding that the root cause of mental illness is neurobiological and not sinfulness. Decades of compelling scientific research have made it clear that suicidal behavior is mediated by a complex chemical process in our brains involving the neurotransmitter serotonin, chemically known as 5-hydroxytryptamine or 5-HT.[5] Serotonin is a brain neurotransmitter that is critical to mental health, as it moderates both our experience of stress and anxiety and promotes patient coping.[6]

The National Alliance on Mental Illness (NAMI) cites US federal government epidemiological research revealing that mental illness is common, with nearly forty-four million US adults (one in five) experiencing mental illness each year.[7] Citing additional National Institute of Mental Health research, NAMI also reports that suicide almost always co-occurs with symptoms of psychiatric illness (i.e., more than 90 percent of the time). The role of serotonin in suicide and the statistical link between psychiatric illness and suicide are settled science, based on rigorous empirical research. These are not opinions, fringe medical notions, or philosophical positions, yet they are not well known to the general public or our clergy and lay pastoral leaders. Educating ourselves and our parish communities in mental health literacy will help to change this, and in the process help our parishes to become more responsive.

CATHOLIC MENTAL HEALTH MINISTRY

One such method of cultivating mental health literacy is Catholic mental health ministry, the goal of which is to help create a more inclusive and welcoming Church.[8] Indeed, mental health ministry follows the assertion that the Church's call is to meet those with mental illness, to learn to love them with the love and the passion of Jesus, and to offer them a place of belonging.

Unconditional Christian love evidenced through prayerful accompaniment is one element of Catholic mental health ministry. We see our brothers and sisters struggling with mental illness not only as people in need of our help but also as people with whom all of us desire to share communion. Indeed, our brothers and sisters can offer new life and a refreshed spirituality.

Fr. Greg Boyle, who spent most of his career as a priest and spiritual leader in the gang-associated neighborhoods of East Los Angeles, was once asked by a prominent protestant pastor to speak to his "gang ministry" and share how he was able to bring young LA gangsters closer to Christ.[9]

Instead, Fr. Greg shared with his colleague that *he sees* the face of Christ in each and every gang member to whom he ministers. Fr. Greg explained to the lay ministers that by welcoming gang members, praying with them and accompanying them, gang members *bring him* closer to Christ.

Similarly, in Catholic mental health ministry, we do not seek to "cure" our brothers and sisters afflicted with psychiatric illnesses but rather to walk with them as prayerful companions and welcome them into our parish communities.

MINISTRY, NOT TREATMENT

As discussed earlier, mental health literacy is an essential element of Catholic mental health ministry and refers to a basic understanding of current scientific knowledge of the causes, types, signs, symptoms, and treatment of psychiatric disorders. Understanding that mental health ministry is not curative is also part of solid mental health literacy. Indeed, we do not expect our brothers and sisters with cancer to be "cured" before they can participate in parish life. Therefore we hold no such irrational expectations for our sisters and brothers with mental illness.

The mental health ministry must be active in order to be responsive. As such, a Catholic mental health ministry includes a regular program (e.g., monthly) of parish-based events and activities such as speakers, prayer services, and mental health information fairs, as well as a referral system for information about licensed mental health providers. The mental health ministry does not provide treatment, but it is connected to a network of vetted and Catholic-friendly mental health practitioners that are licensed and qualified to provide treatment.

ACTIVE SUPPORT FROM CLERGY IS ESSENTIAL

In support of the mental health ministry is a team of dedicated and trained ministers that may comprise clergy or laypeople. Many deacons are involved in this ministry, as are many laypeople. Importantly, there needs to be a lead for each parish mental health ministry team that is authorized by their pastor to implement this ministry.

At the diocesan level, the support, both vocally and materially, of the bishop is also critical to the success of the ministry. Ideally, the bishop should dedicate personnel and funding for the diocesan-wide coordination and training for mental health ministry. Training for mental health ministry members should include mental health literacy as well as training in the methods and tools available for mental health ministries, such as how to conduct prayer services, small-group discussions, referrals to suitable mental health professionals, and prayerful accompaniment.

OVERCOMING IRRATIONAL FEAR OF MENTAL HEALTH MINISTRY

Unfortunately, we have observed fear and hesitance to embrace Catholic mental health ministry at both the parish and diocesan levels. One irrational fear we have confronted is that somehow the endorsement and implementation of Catholic mental health ministry will expose the diocese and/or the parish to liability in the event of a suicide or violent behavior of a participant in the mental health ministry. In reality, parishioners are dying by suicide every day, and it is possible that those participating in mental health ministry may still die by suicide. Similarly, most violence is committed by people without mental illnesses, and most people living with mental illnesses are no more violent than the general population. In fact, people with severe mental illnesses are much more likely to be victims of violent crime than the general population.[10]

The fear held by some clergy of establishing a mental health ministry is akin to prohibiting the creation of a health ministry or healing prayer group because participating parishioners diagnosed with cancer may die. Mental health ministry is not a cure for mental illness, and we make no such claims. Rather, it is a ministry that embraces parishioners with mental illness and welcomes them into parish life in a way that educates all of us and supports those of us struggling with mental illness.

The fear of liability associated with mental health ministry is rooted in a basic misunderstanding of the ministry. We are not called to become a community of psychotherapists. Instead, we are called to walk side by side with our brothers and sisters dealing with psychiatric disorders and welcome them into a faith community of persistent and patient love. Psychiatry, clinical psychology, and mental health counseling each have their place, but their tasks are different from yet complementary to the tasks of the Church. Our task is to give people back their names and to not refer to them as their diagnoses. Our task is to give them a community to join.

A NEW STORY—UNDERSTOOD AND SUPPORTED

Let's now revisit Tim's case. However, this time let's reimagine how his family would be treated if there were a Catholic mental health ministry in their parish. As we know from the preceding pages, Tim was a thirty-two-year-old single man, college educated and professionally employed, who died by suicide after struggling with severe depression since high school. He is from a devout Catholic family; Tim's parents and siblings meet with their parish priest to arrange the vigil prayer service, Mass, and burial. The family members are distraught, and the priest offers sincere condolences. Additionally, the pastor has invited the parish deacon, who leads the parish mental health ministry, to also meet with the family.

Both the pastor and the deacon have completed basic education in mental health literacy, such as training programs developed by Mental Health First Aid USA, and understand that death by suicide can be a complication of certain psychiatric disorders, such as major depressive disorder.[11] They also understand that most severe psychiatric disorders have a root neurobiological cause and generally require medical, psychological, and behavioral treatments. They share this understanding with the family in a warm and nonjudgmental way. The deacon shares that he lost a younger brother to suicide during the course of a bipolar disorder several years ago.

The pastor offers to weave in themes of suffering, spirituality, and hope into the homily for the funeral Mass. The pastor then asks the family if they want him to discuss Tim's mental illness and death by suicide in the homily. After some discussion, the family concludes that it would be consoling for them and helpful for the community to be open about Tim's struggle with mental illness and his death by suicide; however, they ask that it only be briefly mentioned and not be the focus of the homily. They want Tim to be remembered for his deep faith and how he loved his family. The pastor readily agrees.

The deacon also shares prayers to saints who are patrons for mental health and psychiatric disorders, and then he offers to pray with the family members. Finally, the deacon offers to meet with the family in the weeks after the funeral to share additional information about mental health treatment resources, upcoming mental health ministry activities, and support groups in the parish.

In this reimagined encounter, Tim's family leaves the meeting feeling supported, understood, and included as a cherished part of the faith community. Additional information about Catholic mental health ministries can be found in our book, *Catholic Mental Health Ministry: Guidelines for Implementation* available at www.sandiego.edu/cimhm.

KEY POINTS

- Catholics are often reticent to seek professional mental health treatment, and this interferes with our individual spiritual lives as well as hinders our coming together in communion as a parish community.

- A parish response to suicide is often well intentioned but misguided due to inadequate mental health literacy.
- Mental health literacy involves becoming knowledgeable (or literate) about mental health. It begins with understanding that the root cause of mental illness is neurobiological and not caused by sinfulness.
- A mental health ministry meets those with mental illness, loves them with the love and passion of Jesus, and offers them a place of belonging.
- In a mental health ministry, we do not treat people with psychiatric illnesses; we walk with them as prayerful companions and welcome them into a faith community of persistent and patient love.
- When there is a suicide, a parish with a mental health ministry is better prepared to help the family feel supported, understood, and included as a cherished part of the faith community.

ASK YOURSELF

1. What are my reactions, perceptions, and beliefs about suicide?
2. How does my parish currently support a family when there has been a death by suicide? How could this be improved?
3. What do I need to do to increase my mental health literacy?
4. What mental health issues has my parish encountered? Are there common themes of mental health challenges my parishioners face?

14.

Loving Outreach to Survivors of Suicide

Fr. Charles T. Rubey
Archdiocese of Chicago

Catholic Charities of the Archdiocese of Chicago supports the Loving Outreach to Survivors of Suicide (LOSS), a nondenominational program that assists individuals who are grieving the loss of a loved one by suicide. LOSS offers safe, nonjudgmental environments where survivors of suicide can talk openly about feelings and experiences. It helps survivors find community, direction, and resources for healing. Though the LOSS program is supported by Catholic Charities, it serves people of all backgrounds, as this type of traumatic grief transcends belief systems, cultures, races, genders, and ages.

STARTED BY FAMILIES JOINING TOGETHER

I began my work with survivors of suicide in April 1979. I was working for Catholic Charities of the Archdiocese of Chicago as director of mental health programs, and I was approached by three couples who met one another in a support group for parents who had lost a child. These three families felt bonded with one another, as they had each lost a child to suicide and were finding that their experiences were complex. They struggled to find some type of answer as to why their children died by suicide.

These three couples became friends because of the bond they formed around their losses. Not only did they have the common experience of losing a child by suicide but other similarities also drew them together. They felt comfortable with one another because they did not have to pretend or hide anything. They could be themselves around one another because they shared the intense pain of similar experiences. The comfort level was palpable. As these couples became dear, lifelong friends, they started LOSS. Through individual counseling, support groups, outreach, and education, the LOSS program has grown over the past forty years from supporting three couples to serving thousands of individuals who have experienced a loss to suicide.[1]

STRUGGLING WITH "WHY?"

When compared to other illnesses such as heart disease or cancer, suicide is, of course, strikingly different. Survivors of someone who has died from cancer know why that person died, and they often know approximately when their loved one will die. On the other hand, there is a myriad of reasons why people take their own lives, and their suicide is nearly always sudden and unexpected. Most people who die by suicide do so as a result of some form of mental illness, but not everyone who suffers from mental illness dies by suicide. Two people can have the same type of mental illness, with the same intensity, and one dies by suicide and the other continues to live and struggle with the illness. Why did one person die while the other did not? There really is no answer to this fundamental question.

Survivors live with the painful mystery of their loved one's death. They never know precisely why. The mental illness that ends in suicide can be chronic or brought on by a single traumatic experience, such as the breakup of a romantic relationship. A tragic accident or other event can lead to a severe period of depression or acute anxiety that ends in suicide. While those who grieve the loss of a loved by suicide might have known well the struggle that led to the death of their loved one, they can never know for certain why, which, of course, complicates their grieving.

Some circumstances further complicate the grief journey. An example of this is when a couple loses their only child. There was a group of friends who socialized a lot. They were invited to one another's weddings and spent a lot of holidays and vacations together—sometimes all together, and sometimes in smaller groups. One of the couples had a son who was married and was expecting his first child. The women got together for lunch and dressed up as grandmothers, because this was the first grandchild within the group. But there was one woman in attendance who had lost her only child, her son. She and her husband would never be grandparents. She tried to join in with the laughter and gaiety but was hurting deeply. She shared with me this situation, and I was able to connect her with another woman who had lost her only child. The two connected because of their common experiences, and they offered each other support.

Losing an only child presents a unique type of grief. Social events often begin by talking about the accomplishments of one's children. People who are childless find such situations very awkward. To connect survivors with other survivors who live in similar circumstances can be very helpful from a therapeutic point of view.

CLEARING UP MISCONCEPTIONS

There are many misconceptions about suicide, and part of the role of those working with survivors is to address these.

Many people are under the impression that suicide is a cowardly act or that it is a selfish act. It is neither of those things. Rather, it is an act of desperation. It is a clear message that this person could no longer tolerate the pain of his or her life, and that they saw no therapy or medication that could take the pain away. Many of those who take their own lives see death as the only way out.

People who complete suicide think differently than those of us who do not. If this suffering person had an inkling of the impact their suicide was going to have on their loved ones, they would not end their lives. They don't want to hurt their family members or close friends. They just want to get out of their pain.

I worked with a woman who had lost her husband by suicide, and some of their friends concluded that the marriage must have been threatened. This woman was deeply hurt because nothing could have been further from the truth. Actually, the marriage was very strong, yet the husband suffered from a severe form of depression. He suffered for years from this illness and no one but his wife knew about it. Both kept the illness from their circle of friends due to the stigma surrounding it. When this grieving widow heard about the rumor that their marriage was troubled, she was deeply hurt, especially knowing that her group of close friends had come to this conclusion.

MISCONCEPTIONS IN THE CHURCH

Unfortunately, there are misconceptions and erroneous information about suicide within the Catholic Church as well. I have known a number of people who have lost a loved one to suicide who approached their parish priest to request prayers for their loved one who died as well as for themselves and other members of the family. The first thing out of the priest's mouth was that their loved one was in hell. This, of course, devastated the survivors.

There is still stigma attached to losing a loved one to suicide and such statements reinforce this unnecessary infliction of additional suffering for loved ones, who are already deeply grieving. Additionally those kinds of statements directly contradict the Church's teachings about our capacity to know another's final judgment and on the culpability of sin when someone dies by suicide. The Church teaches that suicide is an objective moral evil; it is wrong to end one's own life. But because most suicides involve extenuating circumstances, such as mental illness, sinful culpability would seem to be lessened, perhaps even removed entirely. Current thinking in the Church is to emphasize the mercy of God along with a forgiving God as clergy and laity alike respond to suicide.

MAINTAINING RELATIONSHIPS THROUGH RITUALS AND MEMORIES

Rituals are an important part of Christianity and other religious traditions. They can provide comfort and a path to healing for the bereaved. Rituals can be very simple, such as reciting a poem, singing a special song, listening to a favorite piece of music, celebrating Mass, or having a prayer service to remember a loved one who has died by suicide. The role of the ritual is to remember this loved one who has gone to the hereafter.

These rituals are reminders that this dearly departed person is still a part of a family. They are not present in a physical sense, but they still exist and remain a part of the lives of survivors. Survivors struggle in the aftermath of losing a loved one from suicide. A vital person in a family is no longer among the living, and a great void now exists where that person once was. Rituals can help make the void less painful to face. Rituals can help partially fill that void with memories and love that make that person present to us in new ways.

Rituals to help the grieving can be religious or secular. They can be as simple as keeping a lighted candle next to the picture of the one who has died. A comforting ritual can be listening to their favorite song. A ritual provides a setting wherein this loved one is remembered. Such rituals are reminders that the loved one remains a part of a family, a friend group, a faith community. A tragedy worse than this person's suicide, if one can imagine something worse, is if they are forgotten. As long as there are rituals to remember this loved one, then they will never be forgotten.

A ritual can be created for the occasion of a loved one's birthday. That particular date has always been important, and after that person dies, the date still has a very significant meaning. The ritual should be an appropriate way to remember that loved one, such as singing or playing that person's favorite song. The ritual could also be a reading that describes that person in a very special way. For example, one family gathers at a different home each year on the occasion of their loved one's birthday to share their loved one's favorite foods. In this way the person is fondly remembered.

It is important to make sure family members support the ritual and are comfortable with it. A young woman had lost her nephew to suicide. She was going home to celebrate Thanksgiving and had prepared a ritual to remember her nephew. The parents were there for the celebration, and as people were sitting down for the meal, this young woman announced that she had a ritual to remember Kevin. His father announced that the name of Kevin, the young man who had taken his life, was never to be spoken again. Obviously, the father had not developed any level of comfort with his son's suicide.

Years ago, some people got the idea of developing quilts to give faces to the AIDS pandemic. Organizers believed that people who died from this disease should be remembered and so the AIDS quilts made their way to different cities throughout the United States. Inspired by this effort, I came up with the idea to remember loved ones who lost their battle with the pain of mental illness and died by suicide. LOSS encouraged members to put a picture of their loved one, along with a message of love and respect, on a 12 x 12-inch square piece of cloth. The squares were displayed in a garden type of setting. There were about 150 squares for the display. We then had these squares bunched together and made into quilts.

We currently have twenty-three quilts that are displayed in chapels or other places of worship throughout the Chicago area. We encourage other people to develop squares so that their loved ones can be remembered and prayed for. The quilt project is an ongoing activity, and more quilts will be prepared. Survivors like the idea that their loved ones are remembered in a very special way and are not forgotten.

Telling stories about a departed loved one can make that person present to other people. When Jesus left the earth, his friends and followers were devastated. Each Sabbath they would gather in different homes and tell stories about Jesus and share in the breaking of the bread (the Eucharist). That was one way that they remembered Jesus. Around the year 60, Mark wrote his version of the stories of Jesus. Around the year 70 or 80, Matthew and Luke wrote their stories about Jesus. About the year 100, John wrote his version. That is how early Christians remembered Jesus—by sharing their stories of him and his works. They wrote down the stories. Survivors of loss by suicide can do the same with their loved ones. These stories can be handed down to other generations as a way to always remember their loved one. You need not write them all down, but share the stories.

THE PLACE OF SUICIDE IS HOLY GROUND

Where a person dies is a very holy and sacred place because that is the place where a hurting soul found peace and freedom from the pain and torture of mental illness. It is a sacred and holy place because the person who died there was engulfed by God and is now no longer suffering. Often it helps those who are grieving to bless the place with a special ritual or service that includes scripture reading and opportunities for loved ones to share favorite stories and memories of the person who has died.

I have developed a ritual to bless such places. I have been in garages, bedrooms, basements, and other parts of a house to bless and remind survivors that this place is very sacred and holy because this is where this loved one found their peace and was engulfed by God. It is not a spooky or scary place but a place that should be honored because God embraced their suffering loved one there.

The ritual begins by recalling that we are on holy ground and in the presence of the Father, the Son, and the Holy Spirit. I then generally read the story about Zacchaeus from Luke 19:1–10. The important sentence is when Jesus declares that "today salvation has come to this house." This is the reading:

> Jesus entered Jericho and was passing through. A man was there by the name of Zacchaeus; he was a chief tax collector and was wealthy. He wanted to see who Jesus was, but being a short man, he could not, because of the crowd. So he ran ahead and climbed a sycamore-fig tree to see him, since Jesus was coming that way.
>
> When Jesus reached the spot, he looked up and said to him, "Zacchaeus, come down immediately. I must stay at your house today." So he came down at once and welcomed him gladly. All the people saw this and began to mutter, "He has gone to be the guest of a sinner." But Zacchaeus stood up and said to the Lord, "Look, Lord! Here and now I give half of my possessions to the poor, and if I have cheated anybody out of anything, I will pay back four times the amount."
>
> Jesus said to him, "Today salvation has come to this house, because this man, too, is a son of Abraham. For the Son of Man came to seek and to save what was lost."

I then offer a spontaneous prayer for their loved one and for the survivors and then solemnly sprinkle the spot where the person died with holy water.

As a final blessing, I make the Sign of the Cross over the spot where the person died and conclude with prayer:

> Eternal rest grant unto her (him), O Lord, and let perpetual light shine upon her (him). May she (he) rest in peace. Amen.
>
> May her (his) soul and the souls of all the faithful departed, through the mercy of God, rest in peace. Amen.

It is a simple ritual, but it is very meaningful and consoling to the family members. You can access and adapt for your usage this simple blessing ritual at https://www.avemariapress.com/products/responding-to-suicide.

One of the most unusual places that I have blessed was a railroad track. There, a young woman lost her husband to suicide when he jumped in front of a train. The two of us went out to the place where he jumped and remembered him with a ritual. Such places are sacred and should be respected as such. They can be a physical place of healing for the survivors.

PROVIDING SUPPORT AND CONNECTION

When LOSS began forty years ago, I facilitated two survivor support groups and did some individual counseling with survivors. The program now hosts fifteen monthly support groups at fifteen sites in four dioceses in Illinois and Indiana, relying on dozens of volunteer facilitators who have lost loved ones to suicide and have dedicated their time and energy to helping others heal and regain a feeling of hope. We have a robust counseling program for adults, children, and youth, with seasoned and trained clinicians who understand the complexities of suicide grief.

LOSS also sends out a survivor newsletter each month called *The Obelisk*. It is so named for obelisks of ancient Egypt, four-sided solid pillars that taper as they rise. *The Obelisk* contains writings of survivors and survivor issues. It is a record of struggles that survivors encounter on the journey of grief.

As survivors make their way on the journey, their spirits rise and the intense pain, while it never goes away, begins to taper off. *The Obelisk* and other LOSS offerings strive to lessen that pain and offer a message of hope. *The Obelisk* and other information about the LOSS program can be found on the LOSS website hosted by Catholic Charities of the Archdiocese of Chicago (https://www.catholic-charities.net/GetHelp/OurServices/Counseling/Loss.aspx).

KEY POINTS

- Loving Outreach to Survivors of Suicide (LOSS) was formed to meet the needs of those grieving the death of loved one to suicide.
- It operates under the auspices of the Archdiocese of Chicago but is nondenominational in its programming.
- A major objective for all of us who are pastoral leaders is to end the misconceptions about suicide in society and in the Church in order to reduce the stigma.
- Rituals are an important way to remember our loved ones and to help us in our grief.
- Support groups can help, and professional support needs to be available to help people with difficult complex grief.
- Ongoing communication with a newsletter, such as LOSS's *The Obelisk*, helps people move through their grief and find hope.

ASK YOURSELF

1. What support groups that focus on suicide are available in my area?
2. What misconceptions about suicide have I encountered? How have I responded?
3. What rituals can my parish offer to help people who are grieving a suicide?
4. Am I prepared to lead a family in praying together at the location of their loved one's suicide? If not, what will I do to be prepared?
5. How can I "go the extra mile" to help a family develop their own rituals?
6. How does my parish provide ongoing support and hope to a family that is grieving a loved one's suicide?

15.

Youth Ministry and Suicide

WHAT I LEARNED IN CRISIS

Chris Miller, EdD
Chair of the Council on Mental Illness
National Catholic Partnership on Disability

I have a question for those of you involved in youth ministry: How will you help the young people you serve when there is a suicide in your community? It is likely that you will have to face the issue of suicide at some point—a youth suicide, the suicide of a prominent adult in the community, or the suicide of a celebrity that the young people admire.

I was a youth minister in a community that had five teenage suicides in less than one year, what is called a "suicide cluster." I will describe what we did in the youth ministry of our parish, how our efforts fit into what the broader local community was doing to face the crisis, and some lessons we learned.

I will also share the importance of self-care and the insights that a youth minister can bring to their ministry when they themselves struggle with mental illness. I live with depression and have been hospitalized. I have learned that it is important to be open and honest about our own mental health challenges. The young people we minister to need to see that seeking good medical care is the best way to respond when mental illness strikes, and that Christ is with us in the midst of our struggles.

A SUICIDE CLUSTER AND
A COMMUNITY IN CRISIS

In mid-August 2009 I had recently been hired as a youth ministry coordinator for the St. Thomas Aquinas Catholic Community of Palo Alto, California. I had just finished teaching two years of sixth grade at a Catholic school in San Jose and felt called to work with high school students.

Palo Alto, with a population of sixty thousand people, has been long known for its affluence and high-achieving residents, and for being the backyard of the renowned Stanford University. It is one of many communities on the route south from San Francisco to San Jose. These communities provide housing for the people who work for the Silicon Valley giants such as Facebook, Google, Sun Microsystems, and many other very successful corporations.

Caltrain connects the area with five-car, double-decker, diesel-powered trains rolling along at fifty miles an hour throughout the day. In many places, there is only a crossing gate that comes down when the train is due to pass. These crossings, plus Henry M. Gunn High School with its 1,900 students located within hearing distance of the trains, was the setting for the suicide cluster of five young people in the community. According to the Centers for Disease Control and Prevention (CDC), a suicide cluster is defined as "a group of suicides or suicide attempts, or both, that occur closer together in time and space than would normally be expected in a given community." While the exact reasons why suicide clusters occur are unknown, there appears to be a connection to a phenomenon called "suicide contagion," which is a process by which exposure to suicides and/or suicidal behavior by one or more people influences others to attempt suicide.

Beginning in the spring of 2009, the year I first started at St. Thomas, and stretching over nine months, three Gunn High School students, one incoming freshman, and one recent graduate all put themselves in front of oncoming Caltrain trains and died by suicide. Unfortunately there would be an exceedingly rare second suicide cluster of four teens in the Palo Alto community during the 2014–2015 school year.

SEEKING ANSWERS

The suicides in Palo Alto became national news: "The Silicon Valley Suicides: Why Are So Many Kids with Bright Prospects Killing Themselves in Palo Alto?"[1] and "Disturbing Suicide Cluster Prompts CDC to Start Investigation in Palo Alto."[2]

At the same time, the community was looking inward to reflect upon why young people were dying from suicide. Representatives from the school district, nonprofit agencies, health organizations, religious groups, businesses, and the city came together to form the Palo Alto Youth Collaborative, which worked to involve youth in developing programs to strengthen the community.

Although there are no easy or straightforward answers, factors explaining the suicides were the topics of discussion in homes, at government agencies, and among friends. One factor that was discussed concerned mental illness and depression. According to most studies, between 60 to 90 percent of individuals who die by suicide have some sort of mental illness. Another factor concerned stress and anxiety. The burden of living in an area of highly educated, economically successful people plays a role in how community members see themselves. A significant number of parents in Palo Alto have advanced degrees and serve as CEOs or in other executive positions in Silicon Valley tech companies.

Unrealistic expectations are another factor. Young people are taught early on that to be successful, they must go to the best university, which means taking the most rigorous academic courses possible and as soon as possible. Unfortunately, the high expectations put upon students can have negative consequences, including unhealthy stress and often crippling anxiety. In addition, the adolescent brain is still developing, particularly the prefrontal cortex, which is the part of the brain responsible for planning, considering consequences, and impulse control. These factors lead some teens to believe that suicide is the only answer to escape the unrelenting stresses and pressure of having to achieve. All these factors and probably others were at play. Yet the exact reasons for the suicides will never be known.

THE FAITH COMMUNITY RESPONDS

After the third suicide, the faith community in Palo Alto came together and organized a community event, "Supporting Our Teens in a High-Pressure Environment: A Multifaith Community Response." The event featured the mayor of Palo Alto and faith leaders from five communities: Buddhist, First Church of Christ Scientist, Jewish, Muslim, United Church of Christ, and Catholic.

The purpose of the event was to add the unique gifts of spiritual traditions and faith communities as a source of strength and guidance in service to the whole community. Panelists spoke about the need for the faith communities to come together and support young people and their families. Faith leaders expressed their commitment to be involved in future discussions about teen mental health as the community tried to find a way to respond to the suicide cluster. It was an inspiring event at a somber time in the community.

As a result of this event, faith community leaders in Palo Alto, particularly those working with youth and young adults, were invited to become engaged in collaborative efforts with young people through the Palo Alto Ministerial Association. I co-spearheaded an effort to bring youth ministers and pastors together, focusing on how ministers can work to support young people at a spiritual level.

Within the Catholic community, St. Thomas Aquinas Parish hosted a meeting titled "Catholic Response to Teen Suicide: What Can We Do as a Community?" Our parish's pastor and the superintendent of the Palo Alto Unified School District who was a parishioner, spoke at the event.

ONGOING WORK WITH THE COMMUNITY

It would take the community coming together to end this cluster of suicides and to establish ongoing suicide prevention and mental health programs. Education, prevention, and intervention became essential, and I spent much of my time working on community-wide committees.

Project Safety Net was created to develop and implement a community-based mental health plan of education, prevention, and intervention strategies that provided a safety net for youth in Palo Alto. I participated as a representative of the faith community.

Twenty-two initiatives were proposed for Project Safety Net. One effort was to have volunteer watchers monitor the most visible Caltrain intersections. Another mandated a new class that included a mental health curriculum and moving fall-semester finals ahead of winter break so that students would be free from school anxieties over the Christmas season. Faculty members received books on stress relief and relaxation. New counselors were added. A policy to limit homework was adopted.

Although these changes were widely accepted by adults, they were resisted by the students and the students themselves undercut some of these changes. In 2011, Gunn's start time was moved to 8:25 a.m., based upon research indicating that later-morning classes improved sleep, boosted academic performance, and decreased incidents of depression. But students clamored for an optional 7:20 a.m. class, known as "zero period," because they preferred to start school early in order to have more time later in the day for sports, jobs, and other extracurricular activities. Some of the proposals worked, and others did not. These types of proposals are fluid; depending upon the community leadership and major players it is difficult to measure successes and failures.

THE DEVELOPMENT ASSETS FRAMEWORK

In addition to Project Safety Net, the community adopted the Developmental Assets Framework (DAF)[3] created by the Search Institute and supported by Project Cornerstone, an effort of the Silicon Valley YMCA. Project Cornerstone began in 1999 in Santa Clara County as a coalition of community-based organizations: YMCA, YWCA of Silicon Valley, Girl Scouts, Boy Scouts, Big Brothers/Big Sisters, Boys and Girls Club, and Estrella Family Services. I spoke often at community meetings about the importance of focusing on developmental assets. In fact, the United States Conference of Catholic Bishops in their 1997 seminal document on youth ministry in the United States, "Renewing the Vision,"[4] included the framework as a model for youth ministry.

The DAF is available on the Search Institute web page and can be downloaded for free. The framework identifies forty positive supports and strengths that young people need to succeed, also known as protective factors that help offset risk factors. Twenty of the assets are termed "External Assets" that focus on the relationships and opportunities youth need in their families, schools, and communities. The external assets are organized into four groups: support, empowerment, boundaries, expectations, and constructive use of time. The other twenty assets are termed "Internal Assets" and focus on the social-emotional strengths, values, and commitments that are nurtured within young people. The four internal assets groups are commitment to learning, positive values, social competencies, and positive identity.

The Santa Clara County Project Cornerstone linked these developmental asset groups to "eight keys of thriving youth" using the following sentences:

- I mean something to the people in my world (support).
- I make a difference in the world (empowerment).
- I know what's expected of me and what behaviors are "in bounds" and "out of bounds" (boundaries/expectations).
- I have balance in my life between activities that challenge me and activities that refresh me (constructive use of time).
- I like to learn new things (commitment to learning).
- I try my best to "do the right thing," and I believe it's important to help others (positive values).

- I know how to make good choices and build positive relationships (social competencies).
- I feel good about myself, and I have a bright future (positive identity).

Each of the eight statements relates to either an external or internal development asset group. For example, the first statement encompasses the six assets related to the "Support Group"—family support, positive family communication, other adult relationships, caring neighborhood, caring school climate, and parent involvement in schooling.

An effective way to address suicide and mental illness is to have an ongoing discussion about these eight keys and examine what we can do to make a difference in the lives of young people. Indeed, it is well documented that the more developmental assets young people experience, the less likely they are to be depressed and attempt suicide.[5] Search Institute studies of almost three million young people have consistently shown a positive connection between levels of developmental assets and lower rates of depression or attempted suicide—the relationship holds for young people from all racial/ethnic and socioeconomic backgrounds.

ONGOING WORK WITH YOUTH

In our Sunday evening youth group sessions at St. Thomas Aquinas Parish, I tried to ensure that the teens had a safe place to share what they had on their minds, how they felt about the recent suicides, and so forth.

Interestingly, the six members of the teen core team charged with planning our Sunday evening youth group sessions shared with me that they didn't want to talk about the suicides anymore because it was continuously discussed in school and with their parents. They wanted a place to go where they could "get away" from all of the suicide chatter in the broader community—a safe place, such as youth group—where they could learn and talk with one another about relationships, school, typical teenager concerns, and needs. We then attempted to focus our youth group sessions on topics that were relevant to them, such as faith and identity, Catholic morality, and Christian prayer.

Due to the can-do attitude of the people in Silicon Valley, it seems as though it was a top priority to solve the teenage suicide problem, and it didn't matter how the youth felt. I was caught up in this too—until the teenagers on our core team told me what they wanted. The lesson from this experience is that it is so easy to get emotionally involved and do what we think is best because we want to help. However, we need to resist our desires and listen to what the youth want and work with them to integrate what they identify as their needs with our responsibilities to provide science-backed guidance and pastoral care.

In addition to Sunday evening youth group sessions, I helped spearhead an effort to provide opportunities throughout the community for young people to gather on Friday and Saturday nights. The idea was to offer relaxing things to do on the weekends and venues for them to connect with one another and with adults. Titled "Friday Night Lights," the series included movies and karaoke nights. In addition to activities planned at the Catholic church, there was a "Teen Open Gym" night at the Palo Alto Family YMCA, and on one Friday about 150 teens turned out for a DJ dance party at the Oshman Family Jewish Center. The people of Palo Alto realized that a community effort was needed to reduce the suicides, and they came together to do this.

Even through the work continued with these projects, there was another cluster of youth suicides in the 2013–2014 school year. The community continues to advocate for greater resources around mental health and suicide prevention.

THE IMPORTANCE OF SELF-CARE

In 2013, I moved across the country to study in a post-master's program in youth and young adult faith at Boston College, and I took a job at a Catholic boarding school in Connecticut teaching theology and serving as campus minister, dorm parent, and soccer/rowing coach—for me, it was a dream job. As the day of my departure from Palo Alto and moving cross country loomed, I became increasingly anxious about the experience, but I attributed most of that to normal nervousness one feels when making significant life changes.

Upon arriving in Connecticut in mid-August, I began to pull together new life—applying for a Connecticut driver's license, furnishing the school-provided studio apartment in the dorm, preparing lesson plans, and setting up the campus ministry office. I was ecstatic to live my dream of serving as director of the campus ministry! The best part of the job was the relationships I was able to build with students—there is something remarkable about the energy and authenticity of high school students.

The upheaval of the move to Connecticut led me to reflect on who I truly was, and I was terrified of what I would find out. As part of my theology teaching position, I was asked to teach sophomore-level Catholic theology and senior-level New Testament. The first unit of instruction for the sophomores focused on the purpose of religion, and I recall teaching a lesson about how a belief in God can help people through experiences of tragedies and tough times. There were a few times while preparing lessons when I struggled to understand how God could truly be present during times of suffering.

Although the work was fulfilling and I was doing well at Boston College, I was very, very sad to the point of feeling complete despair and thoughts of suicide kept coming up. I reached a point when I was at such a low place that I was admitted to the psychiatric unit of the local hospital for fear of harming myself. The six hours I spent at a Connecticut hospital was a terrifying experience, one I never want to relive.

I was discharged after the doctors recognized I was not in danger of hurting myself, and I spent the night in my dorm room at the school. The next day I met with the headmaster of the school, who agreed that a two-week break from the school would be helpful. During this break I decided, with mutual support from the school, it would be best for me not to return to the boarding school, and I flew back to Silicon Valley. It was very challenging to leave the school without saying goodbye or providing closure to the students I worked with and got to know.

The next six months were a severe struggle for me. I realized I had a major depressive episode brought on by the significant life change of moving across the country. Thankfully, through the support of my family and friends, a talk therapist, emotional support groups, a spiritual director, medication, and a personal fitness trainer, I was able to recover from the grasp of depression.

I got to a point where I was able to function by myself and resume normal activities. I was accepted into a doctoral program in education at the University of San Francisco. By October 2014, I was offered a job as a youth minister and was well on my way to putting my life back together.

SHARE YOUR STORY

As I became emotionally and mentally stable, I started exploring ways that I might help others based on my experiences, knowing that God was journeying with me along the way. I am now fully committed to making a difference in the world of mental health ministry, education, and advocacy.

While I could cognitively understand in 2009 why a young person felt compelled to die by suicide, it was not until I had my own mental health crisis in 2013 that I could genuinely understand the grasp that depression can have on one's life; it alters clear thinking. I do not want to relive my experiences with severe depression, but I have come to realize, through God's grace, that the experiences have taught me to be more understanding and sympathetic to those struggling with severe depression and suicidal thoughts.

TIPS AND SUGGESTIONS FOR YOUTH MINISTERS

There are three crucial areas for youth ministers and others working with young people to learn about: prevention, intervention, and postvention.

Prevention

In the prevention category, don't be afraid to talk about suicide with young people. It is well established that talking about suicide and sharing good medical information about suicide does *not* put the idea in people's heads. It actually gives permission for individuals who may be suicidal to talk about it.

It is important that youth ministers are attentive to potential warning signs of suicide. Some key signs include

- threats or talk about suicide
- unexpectedly giving away personal possessions
- decline in school attendance or performance
- withdrawal from usual social contact
- dramatic behavior changes
- previous suicide attempts
- preoccupation with death
- drug and alcohol abuse
- recent move or loss
- running away
- depression, including sadness, crying, helplessness, sleep, and eating disturbances

Take time to listen to young people and show that you care about them. Be willing to talk with them and share your feelings. Consider exploring the "eight keys of thriving youth" described earlier with young people. Get to know them and their dreams and hopes.

In their Developmental Relationships Framework, the Search Institute has identified five elements that make relationships powerful in young people's lives.[6] The five elements are: challenge growth, express care, provide support, share power, and expand possibilities. These elements are expressed in twenty specific actions. The Developmental Relationships Framework can be helpful in assisting youth ministers to develop strong, healthy relationships with young people. Developmental relationships are close connections through which young people discover who they are, cultivate abilities to shape their own lives, and learn how to engage with and contribute to the world around them.

Intervention

In the intervention category, it is important to know the scope of one's work. Most youth ministers do not have the training to provide professional counseling. An excellent book on the role of youth ministers is *Helping Teens with Stress, Anxiety, and Depression: A Field Guide for Catholic Parents, Pastors, and Youth Leaders* by Roy Petitfils.[7]

If a young person is at immediate risk to him- or herself, be sure to assist them in seeking medical attention as soon as possible. Youth ministers need to be aware of any mandated reporting requirements and parish/school and diocesan policies. Some states require reporting if there is a threat of imminent physical harm to oneself or others. It is important to directly ask youth if they are at risk of ending their life, persuade them to get help, and refer them to a mental health professional. The National Suicide Prevention Hotline (1-800-273-8255) and the Crisis Text Line (741-741) are helpful resources to know. Prayer can be very powerful in times of crisis.

Postvention

A good friend of mine is fond of saying "good postvention is good prevention." It is important for youth ministers to be accessible and willing to talk about suicide after a non-fatal or fatal attempt. Having a referral list of mental health professionals can be very helpful. Consider bringing groups of families together to share their thoughts and experiences, and don't be afraid to reach out to other youth ministers in your community. Prayer can be very helpful as well.

The Dougy Center: The National Center for Grieving Children and Families offers several tips for helping youth experiencing a loss to suicide. The following are some tips:

- Allow for a variety of emotional reactions.
- Tell the truth.
- Provide compassionate listening.
- Support routines and consistency.
- Offer choices.
- Provide space for play and creativity.
- Remember the person who died.
- Provide support at school.

- Be aware of words.
- Address stigma.
- Remind our youth that Christ is always with them—they are never alone.[8]

Suicide is not an easy topic to discuss. However, youth ministers must be prepared for the discussion. It is important that we engage in meaningful and substantive discussions with youth on suicide.

The Council on Mental Illness of the National Catholic Partnership on Disability issued a statement, which I coauthored, about the Netflix series *13 Reasons Why*. This was a popular but disturbing show that focused on the suicide of a high school student. I will conclude with excerpts from that statement:

> It is crucial that we let the youth know that they are loved, and they are not alone. Studies show that talking about suicide does not increase suicide attempts, but rather encouraging dialogue makes people feel safe in talking about issues that lead them to despair. We must pray for our youth and young adults and we must be willing to have the important, albeit uncomfortable, conversations that may arise.
>
> The Catholic Church recognizes that human life is sacred and every person is created in God's image. Since all people are created in the image of God, their dignity and worth cannot be diminished by any condition, including mental illness. The reality is over 90 percent of those who attempt suicide struggle with some sort of mental illness, and suicide contagion (exposure to suicide or suicidal behaviors) is a real concern. Fortunately, there are a number of resources available on the web for families, clergy, pastoral ministers, educators, and other caring adults to utilize in learning how to respond in working with youth, and other important factors and issues.

Christ's healing love is present in all things, including mental illness and suicide. The Church can provide hope and a healing presence for young people with mental illness. We can accompany them, check in with them and ask them how they are doing, and pray with them and help bear their burdens.

KEY POINTS

- It is likely that a youth minister will have to face the issue of suicide at some point.
- Get involved in your community's suicide prevention efforts so that you can add the unique gifts of the Catholic Church as a source of strength and guidance in service to the whole community.

- Learn about prevention, intervention, and postvention and educate yourself on tools to help youth, such as the Developmental Assets Framework that identifies forty positive supports and strengths that young people need.
- Remember the importance of self-care, and be willing to share your personal journey and experiences in service to assisting the youth you serve.
- Remind youth that Christ is always with them—they are never alone.

ASK YOURSELF

1. Do I know someone who attempted suicide? How did I respond emotionally, spiritually, and physically?
2. How do I and my parish or school recognize and value our youth?
3. What is our plan to help students who show warning signs of mental health struggles and suicidality? What are the reporting requirements I am obliged to follow when there is a threat of imminent physical harm to oneself or others?
4. How might I share stories about my own mental health struggles or those of a loved one?
5. What do I do to take care of my own mental health?
6. What community resources can I enlist to help the young people I work with who are experiencing mental health issues or grief because of a suicide?

16.

Journey from Suicide Loss to Assimilation

Tom and Fran Smith
Karla Smith Behavioral Health
Belleville, Illinois

Our twenty-six-year-old daughter, Karla, died by suicide on January 13, 2003. More precisely, her bipolar disorder took her life, as cancer or heart disease takes many other lives. The experience of the Shoener family as described in chapter 3 of this book mirrors our story in most of the basic facts leading up to and immediately following Karla's death. Many of the emotions the Shoeners described we also felt, thirteen years earlier.

Our faith and parish community also soothed our stricken souls and played a major role in gently moving us from devastating loss to assimilating her death into the rest of our lives, which is how we describe our current status. For us, assimilation means that we can fully participate in our daily lives: laughing at a joke, planning our next road trip, playing cards with friends, discussing politics, meditating in the morning, and even facilitating our support group meetings without an overwhelming sense of loss because of her death. We figure that's as good as it gets.

WE GRIEVE DIFFERENTLY, TOGETHER

Those early grief emotions—shock, loss, guilt, anger, frustration, rejection, depression, loneliness—were unique in their intensity and attacked us simultaneously, like a pack of snarling wolves. We responded to this onslaught of feelings differently—Fran needing to talk about them, and Tom wanting to isolate. She had a lot to say; he couldn't find his words.

It took some months but, once we identified what was going on, we learned to respect each other's approach to this kind of grief. Eventually Tom found some words to express his reactions, initially through writing in a journal and then writing a book about this family tragedy (*The Tattered Tapestry*). And she talked with others until Tom could untie the tangled emotional knots and join her. In time, the wolves slinked away, disappointed, and searched for more vulnerable prey.

KARLA'S FUNERAL STARTED OUR HEALING

The initial response to Karla's death from our diocese and parish was outstanding and comforting. Everyone knew how she died. Tom was the director of pastoral services for the Diocese of Belleville, Illinois, and Fran was principal of Queen of Peace Catholic Elementary School. Bishop Wilton Gregory (now archbishop of Washington, DC) cancelled a diocesan pastoral council meeting to participate in the funeral Mass and say some compassionate words.

Our pastor and friend Fr. William (Bill) Hitpas was the celebrant and preached a remarkable homily on God joining us in our loss and pain. Kevin, Karla's twin brother and only sibling, spoke after Communion with a moving letter he wrote to his sister and invited the attendees, group by group—grievers from Oklahoma, Iowa, New Jersey, Wisconsin, and our local southern Illinois area—to rise in tribute to her life.

The liturgical experience took us from our individual, private misery and gently engulfed us with care, understanding, a tangible presence of God, and the love of Jesus. That immediate tangible response has continued in multiple ways through the next sixteen years.

OUR CALL TO HELP OTHERS

Many people who came through the condolence line at Karla's wake mentioned that someone in their family or among their friends also struggled with mental illness or died by suicide. Both of us, plus Kevin, were surprised at how frequently we heard these comments.

We decided then and there that we needed to do something about it. We pledged, with Karla in her coffin behind us, that we would create a way to assist people affected by mental illness or suicide and their families. Through the creative advice of a number of professionals, including our friend Fr. Charles T. Rubey and his Chicago-based LOSS program as described elsewhere in this book, we gradually refined our mission to supporting families affected by mental illness and suicide. Two years later we formed a nonprofit organization now called Karla Smith Behavioral Health (KSBH) (www.karlasmithbehavioralhealth.org) to fulfill that pledge.

What we learned through KSBH and its many services is that a ministry like this provides concrete help for thousands of people, but it is also an emotional and spiritual resource for us. Through prayer, spiritual direction, and meditation we have come to see that serving others with these issues is our personal and specific way to live out the Gospel message to love our neighbors, especially those in need. Fran provides a mentoring service to many people struggling with issues related to mental illness and suicide loss, while Tom is active as a member of the board of directors and does multiple public presentations on these themes. While our organization is not a designated Catholic ministry, we are comfortable in thinking about it in those terms. The secular and the sacred intermingle especially in terms of service to others.

OUR PARISH SUPPORTS OUR FAITH, OUR GRIEF, AND OUR OUTREACH

Over the years, our parish community has consistently enriched our growth in faith, nourishing our grief work through multiple individual and group experiences. Fr. Bill became a compassionate and effective spiritual director and counselor, offering insight into the grief that clouded our judgment about everything and assuring us that even our negative feelings such as guilt and anger were normal.

We have been part of a small faith group sponsored by the parish for about twenty years, predating Karla's death. Over these years we have become close friends and shared our life experiences—the death of family members; personal health issues, including cancer; an automobile accident; multiple operations; marriages of children; and births of grandchildren. We meet about twice a month to search for and find how God is present within our lives, comforting us in the sad times and celebrating with us in the good times. Through those friendships we have met the ongoing presence of Jesus. The wisdom in the group reflects the wisdom of Jesus. We have studied our faith, clarifying what we believe, and inspiring one another by sharing our life experiences through spiritual books, videos, and asking the questions that shape our spiritual journeys. We are not alone.

Many of the people in this small faith group also join a larger gathering each Sunday morning between Masses for our Dialogue with the Word program. Once again, the faith convictions of these people help break open the scripture readings of the day, and we are nourished and guided by the scripture texts themselves but also by the way these devoted Catholics apply that message to their lives. It is another opportunity for us to deepen our trust in the loving presence of our God, who continues to comfort us in our ongoing sense of loss due to Karla's suicide.

There is no getting over our daughter's death but a continuous getting through that grief, even though the most intense part of the loss is thankfully behind us. We still miss her, of course, because a young death means that we grieve the future that will never be. Milestones that will never be experienced—a wedding, grand-children, her husband, her career, all the things she would have done or become. Flashes of what might have been still haunt us. Our participation in the small faith group and the Dialogue with the Word program offer a consistent commu-nity of faith-inspired friends who help cushion the grief and create an accepting atmosphere and a culture of understanding, comfort, and support.

Once a year on the Sunday closest to her date of death, one of the weekend Masses is for Karla. It is a memorial for us and, in a specific way, helps us focus on the Death and Resurrection of Jesus as a prelude to Karla's resurrected life, where the effects of her bipolar disorder no longer interfere with her generous and loving spirit. At this Mass and throughout the year, there are often prayers of intercession with mental health and suicide themes. And Fr. Bill often includes mental illness in his always inspiring and enlightening homilies. We take great comfort in these public liturgical expressions of the compassion of Jesus and the sacramental presence of Christ.

The parish also promotes a unique To Be Given Away program, which is one of the many opportunities to donate to worthy causes as a part of our parish tithing efforts. Everyone is invited to put some of their donation dollars into this program. The result is that parishioners vote on how the gathered money gets distributed to local causes.

Our Karla Smith Behavioral Health organization has received funds each year from this generous and creative program. The support from the Church is not only spiritual and emotional but also financial; it helps us offer our services to more people. In fact, we use that money for scholarships for parishioners who need our help. Our gratitude for this financial contribution is profound and deepens our personal ties to this faith community.

POWERLESSNESS AND ASSIMILATION

We have learned that Karla's death has pushed us into the world of powerlessness. We are haunted occasionally by what we might have done to intervene in her suicide and, in our worst times, have felt guilt and regret for not being there to stop her—possibly. We now know and accept that, all things considered, we did what we could do at the time.

We professed our love for her and told her we would support her and be with her in her deep depression, but in the end, we could not penetrate the darkness of her desperate sense of aloneness. We could not assure her enough that she was not a burden to us that we could not handle.

In the end, she felt alone, a burden, and could see no other way to release the emotional, psychological, and spiritual pain that ate away at her resolve to live. Her suicide was, to her, her only way to relieve her suffering. And at that final moment, we were powerless to change her confused and misguided mind.

We wish we would have learned the depths of this powerlessness some other way. But we now know that we are powerless in other areas of life as well, and this perspective has matured us and guides us in these other areas. We judge others less. We empathize more quickly and at a greater depth. We identify immediately with other suicide survivors.

Our lives have better priorities. We have discovered more depth in our love for each other. Our faith has taken on another dimension. Our work with KSBH is fueled by our desire to lessen the pain suffered by others who are faced with mental illness or suicide.

In the final analysis, we want our daughter back. We are still assimilating. But the last twenty years have taught us some things that we might not have learned. We are grateful for the learning but sad that we learned it in the mental illness and suicide classroom. And we are also thankful that this classroom was in the Catholic school of life.

All of this exposure to our Catholic faith provides us with a constant presence of the core messages of Christianity—the daily awareness of the reign of God as proclaimed by Jesus, the ongoing reality of transforming death into resurrection as initiated by Jesus, the anticipation of a blessed eternal life, the compassion of a loving God, the redemptive potential of suffering, the saving power of Jesus' life and teaching.

These core Catholic teachings are more than consoling and comforting doctrines. They are embodied in our friends, leaders, and faith companions in our parish programs and help guide us to peace, consolation, and the courage to face another tomorrow with confidence and hope. Over the years, this lived message becomes the ocean we swim in and the purified water we drink.

KEY POINTS

- Karla Smith was a beautiful young woman who died by suicide brought on by bipolar disorder.
- We have learned to understand and respect each other's different ways of grieving and have accepted our powerlessness as we assimilate Karla's death into our lives.
- Karla's funeral liturgy took us from our individual, private misery and gently engulfed us with care, understanding, and the tangible presence of God.
- Our parish regularly incorporates prayers for those living with mental illness and who have died by suicide into liturgies. This is crucial to our ongoing journey of fruitful grieving, as it is for many others.
- Our parish has provided support to us in our grief and in our efforts to help others with programs and tangible support in ways that embody our Catholic faith.

ASK YOURSELF

1. How can my parish be better prepared to recognize the needs of families, loved ones of the deceased, and the wider community following a suicide? How will we plan ahead for funeral liturgies and pastoral outreach that offer suitable consolation and communicate the mercy and love of God?
2. How does my parish incorporate support to people living with mental illness and those who have died by suicide into liturgies?
3. How can I encourage parishioners to talk openly about mental illness, suicide, and grief with me and within other groups in my parish? What can I do now to support this effort?
4. How can I help parishioners who are ministering to people living with a mental illness?

Conclusion

THE PRIORITY OF PASTORAL CARE

Bishop John Dolan
Diocese of San Diego

Suicide affects us all. Most adults are aware of someone who has attempted or died by suicide, and as the number of suicides grows, there has been a greater need within our Church to address this reality. The lives of survivors of suicide victims—parents, children, siblings, friends, coworkers, and parishioners—are forever altered. After the suicides of our siblings and brother-in-law, one of my sisters said, "Suicide has become an increased option for me." My answer to that is, "It doesn't have to be an option."

The chapters of this book have touched on the Church's response to the morality of suicide and the stigma and shame that many face when dealing with depression and other psychological disorders and illnesses. They go beyond the mere theological and moral constructs regarding suicide and touch on the raw human emotions surrounding this troubling reality that we are facing on an ever-increasing basis.

Pope Francis's call to *accompaniment* can never be more on point than when dealing with the harsh reality of mental disorders, depression, and suicide. As a Church, we must embrace this challenge to accompany our brothers and sisters who struggle daily with psychological and spiritual desolation. Embracing this challenge means attending as well to the welfare of survivors of loved ones who have taken their own lives.

Accompaniment is an antidote to depression. Daily articles, news bites, and statistical analyses are not enough to curb the hike in suicides. In fact, evidence shows that such reporting may actually have an adverse effect. Copycat suicides seem to occur when stories of celebrities who take their own lives spread across social media. While media portray the sadness of suicide, the Church is taking steps through various ministries and support systems to promote the value of life. Of course, the fullness of life through Christ is always our end goal, and our effort in spiritual and pastoral accompaniment is the Church's response toward achieving that end.

Pastoral care for those struggling with psychological disorders or mental illnesses and those who survive them is becoming a priority for many dioceses and parishes, as well it should. A great deal of attention, especially in recent years, has been given to Catholic mental health ministry and to addressing the real need to help curb the growing numbers of suicide deaths and to pastorally assist those who have been caught in the tragic wake of a loved one's suicide.

Some of our contributors—myself included—are part of parish, diocesan, and national Catholic mental health networks designed to attend to the spiritual and emotional needs of our loved ones. Accompanying is not easy. It requires patience and a lot of love.

I am grateful to the contributors of these chapters who, through their own patience and love, have offered great insights and helpful practices in addressing this harsh reality found in our families, parishes, and communities. One of these contributors, Deacon Ed Shoener, who initiated this project, has been an inspiration to me. The gifts from him and his wife, Ruth, to the Institute for Catholic Mental Health Ministry at the University of San Diego and the Katie Foundation in honor of their daughter (http://www.thekatiefoundation.org) are their ways of stepping up to the challenge to face the reality of suicide and mental health head-on. His efforts, together with the editorial efforts of Msgr. Stephen J. Rossetti, have made this book a reality. The three of us—deacon, priest, and bishop—and all of our contributors offer to you this book in the hopes that you will know that responding to suicide is not unique to you. It affects us all, and you are not alone!

Appendix 1
SAMPLE FUNERAL HOMILIES

St. William Catholic Church, Round Rock, Texas—March 17, 2017

Homilist—Fr. Jonathan Raia

I think the question that is most often in our hearts, and often on our lips as well, when we're confronted with the death of our loved ones, especially a death as seemingly senseless as Anthony's, is the question "Why?" I know it was certainly the question that was on my heart as I stood with the family a little over a week ago in the garage, praying over Anthony's body.

We know that Anthony had struggled with depression for years, as his journal attests, and talking to Ariana and Leti and the family, we know that in the last hours of his life there was really a fierce battle going on inside Anthony, with the darkness that he described within him.

Knowing that, though, really doesn't make it any easier to deal with his death. That question of "Why?" is still on our lips and still in our hearts—"Why?" What our faith does not try to do is answer that question. Let's make that really clear.

We joked even the night that Anthony died about the well-meaning but stupid things that people sometimes say to those who are grieving. Things like "God took him," or that "it was just his time," or something like that. God didn't take Anthony because he needed him. There's not a bat problem in heaven. (There was a bat flying around at the vigil last night.)

And it wasn't his time. *It was not his time*. And this wasn't the way that the Lord wanted him to go. I think we have to say that. Our faith does not try to answer for us the question of "Why?" The answer that our Christian faith does give to us, the only answer, is the answer that is a Person.

It's the Person of Jesus Christ, God who became man for our salvation. God who suffered and died to free every single one of us from death. It's Jesus, the answer, who when he was on the cross, cried out, "My God, My God, why? Why have you forsaken me?" See, in Jesus, God has said to each and every one of us, "I understand what that 'Why?' feels like. I know it because I felt it too."

The one request that Leticia had for me regarding this homily (she's not afraid to give instructions to priests! I know her, she's not shy), the one request that she had for me was that I proclaim to every one of you that beautiful truth that Noe, who did our second reading, who is such a beloved spiritual father and teacher in this family here at St. William's, that beautiful little saying that Noe loves to preach, "God loves you more than you think he does." God loves you more than you think he does. That was what Leti said: "Tell them that." So, God loves you more than you think he does.

Wherever you are in your own journey of faith, in your relationship with God and relationship with the Church, God loves you today—now. More than you think he does. Much, much, more.

So where was God in Anthony's final days, in his final moments here on earth? Jesus was battling inside of him. Jesus was battling inside of him, giving him the resolve to marry Ariana in the Church, to be a good father to Aaliyah and Camryn. To keep his faith at the center of his life. He wrote those things down. Jesus was right there, and although it might seem to us today that the darkness won that battle inside of Anthony, we are here in this church this morning because we believe that the war has, in fact, already been won.

St. John proclaims to us, "The light shines in the darkness, and the darkness has not overcome it" (Jn 1:5). *The light shines in the darkness, and the darkness has not overcome it.* See, the symbols right now that surround Anthony's body—the paschal candle, the pall—remind us that right over there in that font, seven years ago, Jesus Christ, the light of the world, came to dwell in Anthony's heart. I had the great privilege to baptize him, along with Dan, and Gabe, and Felicity.

And on that night, God the Father looked at Anthony and said, "You are my beloved son. *You are my beloved son.*" The same words that we just heard the Father say to Jesus at the Transfiguration. On that day of his baptism, Anthony received the gift of faith, and Jesus promised him a share in his own victory over death. We are here today to beg the Lord Jesus to remember that promise.

The readings that the family chose are actually the readings that we just listened to on Sunday, the first time that they were here together as a family in this church after Anthony's death. Those were the readings that we heard, and we heard them again this morning.

At the beginning of Lent, every year on the second Sunday of Lent, the Church, after reminding us on the first Sunday that Jesus was tempted, that he battled with the devil—because we all have to—on the second Sunday, the Church gives us this strange and wonderful gospel about the Transfiguration.

See, Jesus knew that he was going to suffer and die. He knew how that experience would devastate his friends, how it would shake their faith to its core. So, on the way to his death, Jesus took his three closest friends up the mountain and gave them a gift. He let them see just for a moment who he really is.

The Church has always understood that in that moment, in revealing the glory of who he is as the eternal Son of God, to those three chosen disciples, Jesus was preparing them. He was preparing their hearts to watch him be mocked, and crowned with thorns and scourged, and executed as a criminal. In the depths of that darkness on Mt. Calvary, he wanted them to remember the light on Mt. Tabor. How the glory of his Father's love for him so filled him that it made him shine like the sun. He wanted them to remember that as they watched him die, so that they could trust that maybe even on that cross, Jesus was still God's beloved son.

But see, the story doesn't end with the Cross. We know that none of what we are doing here today would make any sense if it ended there. The reason that we are here today is that Jesus rose from the dead. Death no longer has any power over him. And in his Church, through Baptism, Jesus has shared that victory with us—his victory over death.

If we allow Jesus to love us, to save us from our sins, and we give our lives to him and live in him, then we too can live forever. That's the hope that we have today for Anthony. That's the hope that the Church gives to each one of us.

So, what does our faith do for us in a time like this? To that question of "Why?"; to the pain and the confusion and the sadness and the anger and the fear and the doubt in our hearts, Jesus says, "I understand. I know. I know what that feels like."

And it's actually there that he's closest to us. *It's there that he's closest to us.* Where maybe we feel farthest away from him, in fact, it's there that he's closest to us, if we have the eyes to see it.

You know, sometimes our Protestant brothers and sisters ask, "Why do you Catholics always have Jesus on the cross? He's risen from the dead." This is why. We keep the image of Jesus crucified always before us so that we will never forget that he understands what it's like.

But it's not only that. It's not just that Jesus meets us in that why. He does something more. Just as he did for Peter and James and John on Mt. Tabor, Jesus offers to us a glimpse of the end game, where this is all headed.

We know that the Jesus on the cross, the Jesus who suffers still with us and in us is also the Jesus who lives forever in heaven with the Father, and who has promised to take us to be with him. That's our hope. Remember at the end of that gospel we just listened to, Jesus tells the disciples to keep the vision to themselves until he is raised from the dead. See, he wanted them to go and give strength to his followers, so that they can know that God knew what He was doing. That the victory was won already when Jesus was there on the cross.

He meant for them to console each other in their trials, in their own experiences of Calvary. To console one another with the knowledge that God can use even this for my good, for my salvation. Because he loves you more than you think he does.

St. Paul understood this. That's why in the second reading we heard, he tells his disciple Timothy, "Bear your share of hardship for the Gospel with the strength that comes from God." That strength is the light of faith that God gives to each one of us at Baptism. It is the light that shines from Jesus on Mt. Tabor, the light that shines from his wounded hands and feet and side, wounds that he still has even in his glorified body. It's the light that God has shown to Anthony's family this past week, through the beauty of this community and faith.

And that light is what we now have to share with Anthony by our prayers. See, we're also here today because we can do something for him. We believe that death doesn't end the bonds that are formed in this life, because love is stronger than death, and so love remains. You and I have a job to do. We commend Anthony to God because we know that God loves him, more than any of us ever could.

Pope Benedict [in his encyclical *Spe Salvi*] had a beautiful image that, in praying for the souls of the dead, the souls in purgatory, we are asking God to put the pieces of their lives back together again. We here today are asking God to put the pieces of Anthony's life back together again. We pray that Jesus' gaze of love and the love of his heart will purify Anthony's heart, to love the way that he was made to love. We pray that the holy pain of that gaze of Jesus' eyes and the love of his heart would cleanse him and really make him truly himself. That's what purgatory is all about: becoming who we truly are in the love of Jesus that purifies us.

So, brothers and sisters, God truly loves you more than you think he does. Jesus came so that you and I would know that love. And even through his Church, Jesus wants to give us the strength to live every moment with the hope that only comes from knowing that Jesus has risen from the dead, that the light shines in the darkness, and the darkness has not overcome it. As we pray that that light will shine upon Anthony and bring him into glory, we pray also that we will live in that same light. We pray that we can know the hope of that light in the trials of our lives, so that we can come to live one day in that same glory.

Amen.

FUNERAL MASS FOR KATIE SHOENER

St. Peter's Cathedral, Scranton Pennsylvania–August 8, 2016

Homilist–Deacon Ed Shoener

Do you all remember the old Louis Armstrong song "What a Wonderful World"? You know the opening line: "I see trees of green, red roses too. I see them bloom for me and you. And I think to myself what a wonderful world."

There is another line in the song that has been running through my mind of over the last few days, and especially this morning, as I look at each one of you. It is this: "I see friends shaking hands and saying how do you do. They're really saying I love you."

Ruth and I and our whole family want to say to each one of you: we so deeply appreciate your kindnesses and simply being present. And so we want to say to my friends in the clergy—Bishop Bambera, Msgr. Rupert, and all the priests gathered here, my fellow deacons—and to all of you—our friends, relatives, and fellow parishioners—we want to add a phrase to that line in the song and say to each one of you: We love you too. Thank you so much.

You know, Katie fought bipolar disorder since 2005, but she finally lost the battle last week to suicide. Katie was so sick with bipolar disorder for twelve years, and despite her best efforts it just got worse. So often people who have a mental illness are known as their illness. People say that "she is bipolar" or "he is schizophrenic." Over the coming days, as you talk to people about this, please do not use that phrase. People who have cancer are not cancer, those with diabetes are not diabetes. Katie was not bipolar—she had an illness called bipolar disorder—Katie herself was a beautiful child of God.

The way we talk about people and their illnesses affects the people themselves and how we treat the illness. In the case of mental illness, there is so much fear, ignorance, and hurtful attitudes that the people who suffer from mental illness needlessly suffer further. Our society does not provide the resources that are needed to adequately understand and treat mental illness.

In Katie's case, she had the best medical care available, she always took the cocktail of medicines that she was prescribed, and she did her best to be healthy and manage this illness—and yet—that was not enough. Someday a cure will be found, but until then, we need to support and be compassionate to those with mental illness, every bit as much as we support those who suffer from cancer, heart disease, or any other illness.

I am not going to even attempt to offer a eulogy this morning. There is no way that I have the strength to tell wonderful stories about Katie and how sweet and vibrant she was. You wouldn't want to see me even try.

What I do want to do, with the strength of the Holy Spirit, is offer a homily that dwells on God's compassionate love. The mystery of God's love and the mystery of Jesus victorious death and resurrection were present in Katie's life and death—and these mysteries are active in our lives as well. We all need to receive consolation and strength to face Katie's death, and one day face our own deaths, with a hope nourished in the saving Word of God.

At this funeral Mass, we pray for Katie because of our confident belief that her death is not the end and it does not break the bonds of love we had with Katie in life. Ruth and I selected the readings we just heard because they speak to Katie's life and death—and how Christ was present through it all.

In the Gospel that I just proclaimed, we remembered the pain of Christ's death. As he hung on the cross, Christ cried out, "My God, my God, why have you forsaken me?" I know Katie cried out those words herself over the past twelve years as she hung on her cross—the cross of a mental illness called bipolar disorder. An evil illness—as evil as cancer and as crippling as MS. But I am deeply comforted by knowing this: Christ was with Katie as she hung on her cross and when she cried out to God, "Why have you forsaken me," just as he is with each one of us as we hang on our own crosses.

And then Crist died—a violent death. Katie's death was violent—a suicide with a gun. Why did Christ allow his life to be taken away, to let himself be crucified? Why did Christ allow this mental illness to take over Katie's life, an illness that so ravaged the most important organ in her body, her brain, that she died by suicide? This makes no sense. Our Church teaches that all life is sacred—from conception to natural death; and so it is.

This is what we believe. We are all made in the image and likeness of God and we were *not* created simply to die. But evil and sin are in the world. Because of evil and sin, we become something less than what God created each one of us to be; something less than the glorious creation that makes each one of us unique and special in the eyes of God. If there was no evil and sin in the world, we would be the immortal beings God created us to be and there would be no death. Yet there is death; it is our last enemy.

But, my brothers and sisters in Christ, death is transformed by Christ's death. Jesus has transformed the curse of death into a blessing. My sister Judy, Katie's godmother, just read to us what the apostle Paul said so many years ago—and what is still so true today. "We will all be changed, in an instant, in the blink of an eye, at the last trumpet." Through Christ, death is transformed, and, like Paul, we can say, "Where, O death, is your victory? Where, O death, is your sting?"

Our answer is that death is swallowed up in Christ's victory over death through his resurrection.

Our faith tells us that Katie will be freed from her pain caused by the terrible mental illness of bipolar disorder, freed from all her fears, freed from whatever attachment she may have had to sin—she will be purified of all of that. She will be purified of anything that made her less than the wonderful, beautiful, vibrant, and holy person that God created her to be.

That is what the Church teaches in the concept of purgatory. It is not a place; it is the process God uses to purify us of all that holds us back, to purify us of all that diminishes us, so that we can be restored to who God made us to be—for Katie to be made whole and glorious so that she, and each one of us, can be with God in heaven.

Her godfather, Joe, read from the ancient book of Lamentations. It is the lament of Ruth and me, and our family, as we walked with Katie in her battle with mental illness these past twelve years. What is said in that scripture is our lament: "My soul is deprived of peace; I have forgotten what happiness is; I tell myself my future is lost. Remembering it over and over leaves my soul downcast within me."

Everyone who has lost a child has told us that it does not get better. Oh, the shock will wear off, but there will always be a pain that will not go away. I guess Ruth and I will have to learn how to live with this—and we will—because God will fill us with hope.

As the scripture Joe just read to us says, "We will call this to mind as our reason to have hope: the favors of the Lord are not exhausted, his mercies are not spent; they are renewed each morning. Our crying and wailing will end—and we will have hope in the Lord. We will wait for the Lord and seek him. It is good to hope in silence for the saving help of the Lord."

Because of these promises of God from ancient times, because of the power and love of Christ's death and resurrection, because of healing presence of the Holy Spirit in our lives each day, I can clearly see that Katie was a beautiful gift from God; that Katie will know the mercy and the love of God.

God loves Katie, God loves each one of us, God loves this world.

Because of God's great love and mercy—well, I can sing to my sweet Katie, I can sing deep in my soul the last lines of that Louis Armstrong song I started with: "I think to myself what a wonderful world, yes I think to myself, what a wonderful world."

Hallelujah and Amen!

Appendix 2
REMEMBERING SURVIVORS OF SUICIDE LOSS IN LITURGICAL CELEBRATIONS

Bishop John Dolan, Diocese of San Diego

These few pages offer some points for liturgical services for survivors of suicide to be held annually or throughout the year in dioceses and parishes. They are offered as suggestions as a means to prayerfully accompany survivors of suicide as they grieve the loss of their loved ones. These services provide added avenues of support for families who are unable to share their stories due to social stigmas related to suicide and mental health.

Services may include Mass, a Liturgy of the Word, or prayers from the Office for the Dead. They may be exclusively Catholic or ecumenical and interreligious in nature. The event may be held on or around Suicide Prevention Day, September 10.

Services may include a procession of roses to a statue of Our Lady of Refuge, intercessions for the deceased members in general or by name, and photographs of the deceased.

Weekday Mass or Liturgy of the Word

On September 10 (Suicide Prevention Day) or at other suitable times, readings may be taken from the day or from the Order of Christian Burial. Prayers and prefaces may be taken from the Roman Missal (*For Several Deceased Persons*).

Sunday Mass on or near Suicide Prevention Day

The Mass might be celebrated within the context of a regular Sunday Mass. The value of offering a Mass for survivors of suicide within a regular Sunday time period gives other parishioners the opportunity to offer support to survivors with their prayers and to witness our Catholic pastoral response to the tragedy of suicide. If

171

held on a Sunday nearest September 10, some homily notes for the Twenty-Third Sunday of the three cycles of the Lectionary are provided here.

A CYCLE—TWENTY-THIRD SUNDAY IN ORDINARY TIME
(Ezekiel 33:7–9, Romans 13:8–10, Matthew 18:15–20)

Being a watchman (Ezekiel) requires patient accompaniment. Catholic parents will lay down general rules for their children and then guide them along in their moral development. Church leaders offer moral precepts, homilies on virtues, retreats, and spiritual direction in order to accompany fellow Christians on their journey with the Lord.

At times, such guidance requires one-on-one conversations with those who seem to be veering off the path. In the Gospel of Matthew, Jesus suggests a three-step approach toward walking a person back to the path of Christ: address the person who has strayed head-on, invite a third party to help intervene, and, if necessary, inform the Church. If the person fails to respond to the three points for direction, Jesus offers a final approach: "Treat them as you would Gentiles and tax collectors," he says. Of course, we know how Jesus treated Gentiles and tax collectors. He dined with them.

Being a watchman requires patient accompaniment. This is especially true as we remember the loss of our friends and family members who struggle with mental disorders alcohol or drug abuse, and who, on their own, can't find a path where they can function properly. In these cases, watchful accompaniment requires many one-on-one conversations of love and support, third-party interventions (counseling, psychiatry, anonymous groups, etc.), and spiritual direction from the Church. After all means have been exhausted, accompaniment must still continue. This is true for those who are gathered as survivors of suicide loss. Not only does the Church and the gathered assembly offer prayerful support for the survivors together with the survivors, but also we accompany those who have died by suicide with our prayers for their eternal repose.

Being a watchman requires patient accompaniment. As a Church, we stand guard with those who grieve, and we keep vigil for those who have died. After all, long before we stood watch over our loved ones, God had a watchful eye over them. Though some struggled to believe in God who could save them, God never stopped believing in them. Maybe they had no hope in the Lord, but God always had great hope for them. And maybe they could not love themselves sufficiently, but Jesus supplied more than enough love for them as they struggled on their journey.

Let us remain watchful and vigilant and entrust these souls to the Lord. May they rest in peace!

B CYCLE—TWENTY-THIRD SUNDAY IN ORDINARY TIME
(Isaiah 35:4-7, James 2:1-5, Mark 7:31-37)

Scripture scholars refer to this passage in Mark's gospel as an example of what is called the "Messianic secret." Found especially in Mark, the secret of Jesus' identity is to be rolled out slowly and deliberately (according to God's time). In the case of the deaf man whose hearing is restored, Jesus' stern warning to keep the miracle a secret is quickly dismissed by the cured man. He shares the matter publicly.

The truth is that we would all probably share the matter publicly. If we were healed in such a way, wouldn't we all want to say who did the healing? Addressing the matter publicly, we would not only say that Jesus cured us. We would also go on to say that he healed us, because he loves us. In this lies the true Messianic secret. God is in love with us.

We all remember the song from the Beatles, "Do You Want to Know a Secret?" It includes the words, "Let me whisper in your ear . . . . I'm in love with you." That is certainly a secret worth bragging about. And, as a Church, we have been proclaiming this secret for over two thousand years.

Unfortunately, as often and loudly as this has been broadcast, many of us still do not hear this voice of Love. Often, those who have died by suicide struggled to know the depth of God's love for them. They struggled to love themselves. This is not true in every case, but for most, their ears were not open to the many voices (including God's) who said, "I'm in love with you."

We know the reasons that may lead a person to suicide. Mental disorder is chief among the reasons for a majority of suicides. Crippling addictions and even situational issues involving breakups or financial distress also lead some to take their lives. Regardless of why, we should make it a point to share the Gospel of love wherever and whenever we get a chance. It should never be a secret. The Messianic secret needs to be proclaimed from the housetops or whispered into the ears of those we love regularly. Let God say, "I'm in love with you!"

As a Church, we also share this Gospel of love with those who have died through suicide. The Mass is offered as a prayer of love for those whose lives ended so tragically. We know that they struggled and were afflicted, but they, like us, are all children of a God of love. There is no judgment here. As the second reading from St. James says, we "show no partiality." We only share love. Love for our brothers and sisters who are deceased, love for their family and friends, and love for all gathered.

C CYCLE—TWENTY-THIRD
SUNDAY IN ORDINARY TIME
(Wisdom 9:13–18; Philemon 9–10, 12–17; Luke 14:25–33)

These words of Jesus in Luke's gospel are hard to grasp. Hating father, mother, children, and siblings? Does he really mean that? It's unimaginable.

Reimagined positively, we understand that loving family and blood relations cannot be made perfect without responding to the call of God who is love. Loving others as we love ourselves flows from the first commandment to love God with our whole heart, soul, and strength. Jesus once said, "Remain in my love" or "Abide in my love" as some translations read (Jn 15:9), so that we might have joy and our joy would be complete. Who wants incomplete joy?

Complete joy comes from putting Christ first always. Remaining in his love brings us joyful fulfillment, which begets greater love from family and friends. Remaining in the love of Christ in Word and Sacrament at Mass is a perfect way to stand with survivors of suicide loss and in prayerful support of those who have gone before us. The Eucharist is the source and summit of the love that we share with survivors and those who have died by suicide. Responding to Christ's call to follow him and to abide in him allows us to find consolation and provide perfect and lasting love and support.

Such a gathering is a response to the pain that family and friends share as they miss their loved ones. It is at events such as these where Christ offers us the peace to endure the pain and to prayerfully consider the mystery of death especially as we contemplate the Death and Resurrection of the Lord himself.

Putting the Lord first, we trust that our loved ones are greeted in the loving arms of Jesus. They now abide with him. He grants them complete joy, without pain of mental disorder, or addictions, or other situational realities that lead them to suicide.

Intercessory Prayers

These intercessions can be used throughout the year, especially during Suicide Awareness Month (September) and Mental Health Month (May) in liturgies and prayer services for those who grieve the loss of a loved one to suicide.

A printable version of these prayers can be found at https://www.avemariapress. com/products/responding-to-suicide

For our Pope, our Bishop, our priests and deacons, and lay Catholic ministers, that they bring the healing presence Christ's peace into the lives of those who are suffering with suicidality and into the lives of those who are grieving a suicide.
We pray to the Lord.

For our elected officials to come to an understanding of the need for laws, policies and funding for effective mental health care and suicide prevention programs.
We pray to the Lord.

For the psychologists, psychiatrists, therapists and all who research the causes of suicidality and provide treatment to people who are suicidal, may God grant them wisdom and compassion.
We pray to the Lord.

For those living with a mental illness, depression, and suicidal thoughts may they find the help and support that they need to lead peaceful and full lives.
We pray to the Lord.

We commend to your mercy and defense all who are contemplating suicide today, right now. Bring someone or something to intervene.
We pray to the Lord.

For families and friends experiencing the loss of a loved one by suicide, may they find healing and comfort.
We pray to the Lord.

For the repose of the souls of the members of our parish, our families, and neighborhoods who have died by suicide. May they experience the mercy and love of Christ.
We pray to the Lord.

We lift up all those who have died by suicide and the fathers and mothers, friends and families who are now living as survivors of suicide.
We pray to the Lord.

Gracious and loving God,
for all the families who have lost a loved one to suicide, bring them
comfort in trusting that your mercy and grace accept their loved one
into the eternal bliss of heaven.
We pray to the Lord.

Appendix 3
PASTORAL POSTVENTION COMPETENCIES

From National Action Alliance for Suicide Prevention: Faith Communities Task Force, *Suicide Prevention Competencies for Faith Leaders: Supporting Life Before, During, and After a Suicidal Crisis* (Washington, DC: Education Development Center, 2019).

To equip faith leaders with the capabilities needed to prevent suicide and provide care and comfort to all those affected by suicide, the National Action Alliance for Suicide Prevention has identified a set of suicide prevention competencies—the recommended attitudes, approaches, and skills for supporting life before, during, and after a suicidal crisis.

1. Pastoral Care Skills

1.1 After a suicide attempt happens, I know how to advise and support friends and family members.

1.2 After a suicide attempt happens, I know how to advise leaders and key members within the congregation.

1.3 When a suicide death happens, I know how to care for the friend(s) and family member(s) of the survivor(s).

1.4 When a suicide death happens, I know how to care for the congregation.

1.5 I ensure that the faith community reaches out to survivors the same way it would support family and loved ones after any death (e.g., casserole suppers, spiritual needs).

1.6 When I talk to survivors, I watch for complicated grief, including guilt, anger, blame, and other mental health issues.

1.7 When I talk to survivors, I allow them to ask difficult theological questions and avoid providing answers to unanswerable ones.

1.8 I watch for people vulnerable to contagion—those closest to the decedent and youth who looked up to the individual.

1.9 I reach out to survivors on anniversaries of events.

2. Skills to Provide Pastoral Care with Awareness of Cultural Differences

2.1 When a suicide death happens, I take the culture of survivors into account— how they experience, display, and process emotions; beliefs about death and the afterlife; rituals to address the death; and comfort level in speaking about the deceased.

3. Knowing and Applying Faith Traditions to Memorial Ceremonies/Services

3.1 When a suicide death happens, I know how to conduct a memorial service or ceremony that is helpful to survivors and congregants while seeking to prevent contagion and increased risk among those attending.

3.2 I conduct or help those doing a eulogy so that it follows guidelines on how to talk about suicide.

4. Self-Care

4.1 I take care of myself to make sure that I'll be emotionally available when needed.

4.2 When a suicide death happens, I am alert and sensitive to the risk of taking on guilt and take steps to avoid doing so.

4.3 I reach out for support when needed.

Appendix 4
RESOURCES

Books

Alar, Chris, and Jason Lewis. *After Suicide, There's Hope for Them and for You.* Stockbridge, MA: Marian Press, 2019.

Barbagli, Marzio. *Farewell to the World: A History of Suicide.* Cambridge, UK: Polity Press, 2015.

Baker McCall, Junietta. *Bereavement Counseling: Pastoral Care for Complicated Grieving.* Binghamton, NY: Hayworth Press, 2004.

Barry, Robert. *The Development of the Roman Catholic Teachings on Suicide.* Notre Dame Journal of Law, Ethics & Public Policy 9, no. 2 (1995): 449.

Bishops of California. *Hope and Healing: A Pastoral Letter from the Bishops of California on Caring for those Who Suffer from Mental Illness Addressed to All Catholics and People of Goodwill.* Sacramento, CA: California Catholic Conference, May 2018.

Calhoun, Lawrence G., and Richard Tedeschi. *Handbook of Posttraumatic Growth: Research and Practice.* New York, NY: Erlbaum, 2006.

Callahan, Wendell J., Liberty Hebron, and Alissa N. Willmerdinger. *Catholic Mental Health Ministry: Guidelines for Implementation.* San Diego, CA: University of San Diego, 2019.

Clemons, James T. *What Does the Bible Say about Suicide?* Minneapolis, MN: Fortress Press, 1990.

D'Arcy, Paula. *Winter of the Heart, Finding Your Way through the Mystery of Grief.* Notre Dame, IN: Ave Maria Press, 2018.

Guntzelman, Joan. *God Knows You're Grieving.* Notre Dame, IN: Ave Maria Press, 2001.

Jobes, David. *Managing Suicidal Risk, Second Edition: A Collaborative Approach, Second Edition.* New York, NY: The Guilford Press, 2016.

Koenig-Bricker, Woodeene. *Meditations for Those Left Behind by Suicide.* New London, CT: Twenty-Third Publications, 2018.

Maris, Ronald W. *Suicidology: A Comprehensive Biopsychosocial Perspective.* New York, NY: The Guilford Press, 2019.

Moore, Melinda and Daniel A. Roberts. *The Suicide Funeral (Or Memorial Service) Honoring Their Memory, Comforting Their Survivors.* Eugene, OR: Wipf and Stock Publishers, 2017.

National Action Alliance for Suicide Prevention: Faith Communities Task Force. *Suicide prevention competencies for faith leaders: Supporting life before, during, and after a suicidal crisis.* Washington, DC: Education Development Center, 2019.

Petitfils, Roy. *Helping Teens with Stress, Anxiety, and Depression: A Field Guide for Catholic Parents, Pastors, and Youth Leaders.* Notre Dame, IN: Ave Maria Press, 2019.

Rolheiser, Fr. Ron. *Bruised and Wounded—Struggling to Understand Suicide.* Brewster, MA: Paraclete Press, 2017.

Ross, E. Betsy. *After Suicide: A Ray of Hope for Those Left Behind.* Cambridge, MA: Perseus, 1997.

Rupp, Joyce. *Praying Our Goodbyes—A Spiritual Companion Through Life's Losses and Sorrows.* Notre Dame, IN: Ave Maria Press, 2013.

Shneidman, Edwin. *The Suicidal Mind.* Oxford, UK: Oxford University Press, 1996.

Smith, Tom. *The Unique Grief of Suicide: Questions and Hope.* Bloomington, IN: iUniverse, 2013.

Vanier, Jean, and John Swinton. *Mental Health: The Inclusive Church Resource.* London, UK: Darton, Longman and Todd, 2014.

Woelfel, Joni. *Meditations for Survivors of Suicide.* Totowa, NJ, Resurrection Press, 2002.

Wolfelt, Alan D. *Finding the Words—How to Talk with Children and Teens About Death, Suicide, Homicide.* Fort Collins, CO: Companion Press, 2013.

Wolfelt, Alan D. *The Wilderness of Suicide Grief: Finding Your Way (Understanding Your Grief).* Fort Collins, CO: Companion Press, 2010.

WEB SITES

Alliance of Hope for Suicide Loss Survivors. https://allianceofhope.org.

American Foundation for Suicide Prevention. I've Lost Someone. https://afsp.org/ive-lost-someone.

Association of Catholic Mental Health Ministers. www.catholicmhm.org.

The Dougy Center, The National Center for Grieving Children and Families. www.dougy.org.

Loving Outreach to Survivors of Suicide. Based in Chicago. LOSS offers hope and healing to those who mourn a loss to suicide. https://www.catholiccharities.net/GetHelp/OurServices/Counseling/Loss.aspx#:~:text=Loving%20Outreach%20to%20Survivors%20of,talk%20about%20feelings%20and%20experiences.

National Action Alliance for Suicide Prevention. Faith.Hope.Life. A campaign aimed at involving every faith community in suicide prevention. https://theactionalliance.org/faith-hope-life.

National Catholic Partnership on Disability. Council on Mental Illness, Suicide. https://ncpd.org/disabilities-ministries-specific-disabilities-mental-illness/suicide.

Nouwen Network: About Suicide. http://nouwen-network.com/aboutsuicide.html.

Suicide Prevention Resource Center: Provide for Immediate and Long-Term Postvention. www.sprc.org/comprehensive-approach/postvention.

Survivors of Suicide Loss (SOSL): Resources. Based in San Diego. SOSL reaches out to and supports people who have lost a loved one to suicide. www.soslsd.org/resources.

Tragedy Assistance Program for Survivors (TAPS) provides comfort, care and resources to all those grieving the death of a military loved one. www.taps.org/suicide.

Waterloo Catholics—Resources for Suicide Survivors. https://waterloocatholics.org/resources-for-suicide-survivors.

Contributors

Adams, Leticia Ochoa is a Catholic writer and speaker who lives in Austin, Texas. She writes about death, grief, trauma, and other fun things on her blog, which she says will "make you laugh, cry, and want to set my blog on fire." Her blog can be found at leticiaoadams.com.

Callahan, Wendell
Executive director of the Catholic Institute of Mental Health Ministry and professor of practice and counseling program director of the Department of Counseling and Marital & Family Therapy in the School of Leadership and Education Sciences at the University of San Diego. Dr. Wendell holds a PhD in clinical psychology with an emphasis in experimental psychopathology from the University of California, San Diego and San Diego State University. He is also a volunteer with the Mental Health Ministry and the Home Ministry at St. Brigid Catholic Church in San Diego, California.

Cordileone, Salvatore J.
Archbishop of San Francisco, installed in 2012 after having served as bishop of Oakland since 2009. Cordileone was ordained a priest in the Diocese of San Diego in 1982. He has a doctorate in canon law from the Pontifical Gregorian University in Rome.

Gonzalez, Dianna
Marriage family therapist in California and writes about grief and healing. Her work is centered around grief and loss and offers individual, family, and group sessions in her private practice in San Diego, CA. Dr. Gonzales facilitates parish based bereavement groups and she works with Rachel's Hope, a Catholic organization to help with after abortion grief support.

Gregory Wilton D.
Archbishop of Washington, DC., installed as archbishop in 2019 after having served as bishop of Atlanta, Georgia,from 2005 to 2019 and bishop of Bellville, Illinois, from 1994 to 2005. Gregory was ordained a priest of the Archdiocese of

Chicago in 1973. He has a doctorate in sacred liturgy from the Pontifical Liturgical Institute in Rome.

Griffin, Carter
Priest of the Archdiocese of Washington, a graduate of Princeton University and a former Naval officer. He completed his doctoral studies in theology in Rome and is rector of Saint John Paul II Seminary in Washington, DC. Fr. Griffin is the author of the book *Why Celibacy? Reclaiming the Fatherhood of the Priest* published by Emmaus Road in 2019.

Hebron, Liberty, LPCC
Lead therapist at the San Diego Center for Children Academy where she oversees the therapeutic services provided to families and children struggling with mental, emotional, and behavioral disorders. She is a faculty member of the Department of Counseling and Marital & Family Therapy in the School of Leadership and Education Sciences at the University of San Diego, where she obtained a master's degree in Clinical Mental Health Counseling in 2014. She is also an active volunteer at her home parish, St. Charles Borromeo in Point Loma, California where she coordinates faith formation for children preparing to receive the Sacraments of Reconciliation and Communion.

Jobes, David
Professor of psychology and associate director of clinical training at The Catholic University of America (CUA) in Washington, DC, and the director of the CUA Suicide Prevention Lab. Dr. Jobes's research and writing in suicide has produced more than one hundred peer reviewed publications, including six books on clinical suicidology. As an internationally recognized suicidologist, Dr. Jobes is a past president of the American Association of Suicidology (AAS).

Miller, Chris
Co-chair of the Council on Mental Illness, sponsored by the National Catholic Partnership on Disability, a member of the California State Mental Health Policy Workgroup, and a member of the National Action Alliance for Suicide Prevention's Faith Communities Task Force. Dr. Miller holds a doctoral degree in education from the University of San Francisco and works as a religious studies teacher at a Lasallian Christian Brothers high school in the San Francisco Bay Area.

Moore, Melinda
Assistant professor in the Department of Psychology at Eastern Kentucky University in Richmond, Kentucky. Dr. Moore serves on the board of the American Association of Suicidology as the chair of the Clinical Division and is the co-lead of the National Action Alliance's Faith Communities Task Force. She published

The Suicide Funeral: Honoring their Memory, Comforting their Survivors (Wipf & Stock) with her coauthor, Rabbi Dan Roberts.

Pope, Charles
Pastor in the Archdiocese of Washington, DC. Along with publishing a daily blog at the Archdiocese of Washington website, he has written in pastoral journals and Catholic magazines. He has conducted weekly Bible studies in the US Congress and the White House. Monsignor Pope was ordained a priest in the Archdiocese of Washington in 1989.

Rossetti, Stephen J.
Priest of the Diocese of Syracuse and an expert on priestly spirituality and wellness issues. He earned a doctorate in psychology from Boston College and a doctor of ministry from the Catholic University of America. Monsignor Rossetti serves as research associate professor of pastoral studies at the Catholic University and a visiting professor at Gregorian University in Rome.

Rubey, Charles
Founder of Loving Outreach to Survivors of Suicide(LOSS), a non-denominational program offered by Catholic Charities of the Archdiocese of Chicago, where Fr. Rubey served as director of mental health services. Founded in 1979 with one small group, LOSS has grown to be a leader in the field of suicide grief, offering support groups and counseling for survivors of all ages, in and around metropolitan Chicago.

Smith, Tom and Fran
Founder of the Karla Smith Foundation, located in O'Fallon, Illinois, supporting families affected by mental illness and suicide across the United States. Tom is author of *The Tattered Tapestry: A Family's Search for Peace With Bipolar Disorder* and *The Unique Grief of Suicide: Questions and Hope.*

Vann, Kevin
Bishop of the Diocese of Orange, California, installed in 2012 after having served as bishop of Fort Worth, Texas,since 2005. Vann was ordained a priest in the Diocese of Springfield, Illinois, in1981.

Willmerdinger, Alissa
RTF Therapist at SpringBrook Behavioral Health in South Carolina where she provides individual and family therapy for youth diagnosed with Autism. She obtained a master's degree in clinical mental health counseling from the University of San Diego.

Notes

Introduction

1. Matthew K. Nock, "Against Suicide: A Century of Little Progress," *Harvard Gazette*, July 21, 2016, https://news.harvard.edu/gazette/story/2016/06/against-suicide-a-century-of-little-progress.
2. Richard A. Friedman, "Suicide Rates Are Rising. What Should We Do About It?" *New York Times*, June 11, 2018, https://www.nytimes.com/2018/06/11/opinion/suicide-rates-increase-anthony-bourdain-kate-spade.html.
3. Friedman, "Suicide Rates Are Rising."

3. The Suicide Death of My Daughter, Katie

1. Colby Itkowitz, "She 'Loved Life': A Grieving Father Wrote Openly about Suicide and Mental Illness in Daughter's Obituary," *Washington Post*, August 17, 2016, https://www.washingtonpost.com/news/inspired-life/wp/2016/08/17/she-loved-life-a-grieving-father-shared-honestly-about-his-daughters-suicide-in-her-obituary.
2. Rui Antunes, "Katie Committed Suicide in a Bipolar Crisis and Her Father Wrote in the Obituary a Message to Humanity," *Visão*, August 26, 2016 https://visao.sapo.pt/atualidade/sociedade/2016-08-26-katie-suicidou-se-numa-crise-bipolar-e-o-pai-escreveu-no-obituario-um-recado-a-humanidade-1.
3. Simone Olivero, "Parents Use Daughter's Obituary to Discuss the Stigmas around Mental Health," *Yahoo News*, August 9, 2016, https://www.yahoo.com/news/parents-daughters-obituary-discuss-stigmas-000000958.html.
4. Sharon Grigsby, "Grieving Father's Commonsense Message about Mental Illness Is a Wake-Up Call," *Dallas Morning News*, August 18, 2016, https://www.dallasnews.com/opinion/commentary/2016/08/18/grieving-father-s-commonsense-message-about-mental-illness-is-a-wake-up-call.

5. Andrea Monaci, "She Loved Life—a Father in Mourning Writes of the Suicide of Daughter with a Mental Illness," *Urban Post*, August 20, 2016, https://urbanpost.it/ha-amato-la-vita-un-padre-in-lutto-scrive-del-suicidio-della-figlia-malata-mentale.

6. Greg Kandra, "On the Deacon's Daughter Who Committed Suicide: 'God Will Use This Death to Help Others Come Out of the Shadows,'" *The Deacon's Bench* (blog), Aleteia, August 17, 2016, https://aleteia.org/blogs/deacon-greg-kandra/on-the-deacons-daughter-who-committed-suicide-god-will-use-this-death-to-help-others-come-out-of-the-shadows.

7. Aimee Meade, "This Father Used His Daughter's Obituary to Make an Important Point about the Way We Treat People with Mental Health Issues," *The Independent*, August 23, 2016, Indy100, https://www.indy100.com/article/this-father-used-his-daughters-obituary-to-make-an-important-point-about-the-way-we-treat-people-with-mental-health-issues-WklKJPqeRDb.

8. "Kathleen Marie Shoener, died 3 August 2016," Legacy.com, https://www.legacy.com/obituaries/name/kathleen-shoener-obituary?pid=180989005.

9. For more development on this, see Ronald Rolheiser, "For Understanding How We Remain in Contact with Our Loved Ones after Their Deaths," in *The Holy Longing: The Search for Christian Spirituality* (New York: Random House, 2014), 104–6.

5.   Priests, Suicide, and Redemption

1. Perry West, "No Different Than the Rest of Us—Priests and Mental Health Care," *Catholic New Agency*, February 15, 2020, https://www.catholicnewsagency.com/news/no-different-from-the-rest-of-us--priests-and-mental-health-care-29239.

2. Katelyn Newman, "Study: Suicide Rates Decline Globally While U.S. Rate Rises, *U.S. News*, February 7, 2019, https://www.usnews.com/news/best-countries/articles/2019-02-07/global-suicide-rate-declines-while-us-rate-rises-study-finds.

7.   History and Pastoral Practice of Catholic Teaching on Suicide

1. Robert Barry, "The Development of the Roman Catholic Teachings on Suicide," *Notre Dame Journal of Law, Ethics & Public Policy* 9, no. 2 (1995): 449.

2. Christopher O'Mahony, *St. Thérèse of Lisieux by Those Who Knew Her: Testimonies from the Process of Her Beatification* (Dublin: Veritas, 1975), cited in J. Linus Ryan, "Suicide: Insights from St. Thérèse of Lisieux," last accessed June 14, 2020, MountainRunner.com, http://www.mountainrunnerdoc.com/page/page/4264578.htm.

3. Sidney Goldstein, *Suicide in Rabbinic Literature* (Hoboken, NJ: Ktav, 1989), 3.

4. Goldstein, *Suicide*, 51.

5. Goldstein, 3.

6. Goldstein, 13.

7. Goldstein, 55.

8. Goldstein, 55.

9. Marzio Barbagli, *Farewell to the World: A History of Suicide* (Cambridge, UK: Polity Press, 2015), 40.

10. Barbagli, *Farewell to the World*, 40.

11. Pliny, *Natural History: A Selection*, quoted in Barbagli, *Farewell to the World*, 330.

12. Barry, "Development of the Roman Catholic Teachings," 463.

13. James T. Clemons, *What Does the Bible Say about Suicide?* (Minneapolis: Fortress Press, 1990), 77.

14. Barbagli, *Farewell to the World*, 41.

15. James T. Clemons, *Sermons on Suicide* (Louisville: Westminster John Knox Press, 1989), 18.

16. Augustine, *The City of God*, bk. 1, ch. 17, trans. Henry Bettenson (London: Penguin Books, 1972). Cited in Barry, "Development of the Roman Catholic Teachings," 467.

17. Barry, "Development of the Roman Catholic Teachings," 473.

18. Barbagli, *Farewell to the World*, 20.

19. Barbagli, 84.

20. Barbagli, 82.

21. Jean-Jacques Rousseau, *On Suicide*, Sophie Project, last accessed June 14, 2020 http://www.sophia-project.org/uploads/1/3/9/5/13955288/rousseau_suicide.pdf.

22. Barry, "Development of the Roman Catholic Teachings," 483.

23. Barry, 487.

24. Ramón Martínez de Pisón, *Death by Despair: Shame and Suicide* (New York: Peter Lang, 2006), 53.

25. Barbagli, *Farewell to the World*, 50.

26. Barbagli, 12.

27. Barbagli, 492–95.

28. Sacred Congregation for the Doctrine of the Faith, *Declaration on Euthanasia*, May 5, 1980, http://www.vatican.va/roman_curia/congregations/cfaith/documents/rc_con_cfaith_doc_19800505_euthanasia_en.html.

9.   Discussing the Hard Questions and Accompanying the Grieving

1. *Hope and Healing: A Pastoral Letter from the Bishops of California on Caring for those Who Suffer from Mental Illness Addressed to All Catholics and People of Goodwill*, California Catholic Conference, Bishops of California, May 2018, https://www.cacatholic.org/hope_and_healing.

2. Stoyan Zaimov, "Rick Warren Praises Catholic Pastoral Letter as 'New Standard' for Mental Health Ministries," *Christian Post*, May 4, 2018, https://www.christianpost.com/news/rick-warren-praises-catholic-pastoral-letter-as-new-standard-for-mental-health-ministries.html.

3. Francis, Lenten Homily, May 18, 2019, "Pope Francis at Mass: Imitate the Mercy of the Lord," Vatican News, March 18, 2019, accessed June 14, 2020, https://www.vaticannews.va/en/pope-francis/mass-casa-santa-marta/2019-03/pope-francis-homily-mass-santa-marta-mercy-lord.html.

10. Suicide Assessment, Treatment, and Prevention

1. Substance Abuse and Mental Health Services Administration, *Key Substance Use and Mental Health Indicators in the United States: Results from the 2017 National Survey on Drug Use and Health*, HHS publication, no. SMA 17-5068, NSDUH series H-53 (Rockville, MD: Center for Behavioral Health Statistics and Quality, Substance Abuse and Mental Health Services Administration, 2018).

2. Substance Abuse and Mental Health Services Administration, *Key Substance Use*.

3. Joseph C. Franklin, Jessica D. Ribeiro, Kathryn R. Fox, Kate H. Bentley, Evan M. Kleiman, Xieyining Huang, Katherine M. Musacchio, Adam C. Jaroszewski, Bernard P. Chang, and Matthew K. Nock, "Risk Factors for Suicidal Thoughts and Behaviors: A Meta-Analysis of 50 Years of Research," *Psychological Bulletin* 143, no. 2 (2017): 187–232.

4. Ronald W. Maris, *Suicidology: A Comprehensive Biopsychosocial Perspective* (New York: Guilford Press, 2019).

5. Edwin Shneidman, *Definition of Suicide* (New York: John Wiley, 1985), 202–13.

6. David A. Jobes and Samantha A. Chalker, "One Size Does Not Fit All: A Comprehensive Clinical Approach to Reducing Suicidal Ideation, Attempts, and Deaths," *International Journal of Environmental Research and Public Health* 16, no. 19 (September 2019): 1–14, https://doi.org/10.3390/ijerph16193606.

7. Hospitalization studies Jobes and Chalker, "One Size Does Not Fit All."

8. Marsha M. Linehan, Kathryn E. Korslund, Melanie S. Harned, Robert J. Gallop, Anita Lungu, Andrada D. Neacsiu, Joshua McDavid, Katherine Anne Comtois, Angela M. Murray-Gregory, "Dialectical Behavior Therapy for High Suicide Risk in Individuals with Borderline Personality Disorder: A Randomized Clinical Trial and Component Analysis," *JAMA Psychiatry* 72, no. 5 (2015): 475–82, https://doi.org/10.1001/jamapsychiatry.2014.3039.

9. Gregory K. Brown, Thomas Ten Have, Gregg R. Henriques, Sharon X. Xie, Judd E. Hollander, and Aaron T. Beck, "Cognitive Therapy for the Prevention of Suicide Attempts: A Randomized Controlled Trial," *Journal of the American Medical Association* 294, no. 5 (2005): 563–70, https://doi.org/10.1001/jama.294.5.563.

10. M. David Rudd, Craig J. Bryan, Evelyn G. Wertenberger, Alan L. Peterson, Stacy Young-McCaughan, Jim Mintz, Sean R. Williams, Kimberly A. Arne, Jill Breitbach, Kenneth Delano, Erin Wilkinson, and Travis O. Bruce, "Brief Cognitive-Behavioral Therapy Effects on Post-Treatment Suicide Attempts in a Military Sample: Results of a Randomized Clinical Trial with 2-Year Follow-Up," *American Journal of Psychiatry* 172, no. 5 (May 2015): 441–49, doi:10.1176/appi.ajp.2014.14070843.

11. Craig J. Bryan, Jim Mintz, Tracy A. Clemans, Bruce Leeson, T. Scott Burch, Sean R. Williams, Emily Maney, and M. David Rudd, "Effect of Crisis Response Planning vs. Contracts for Safety on Suicide Risk in U.S. Army Soldiers: A Randomized Clinical Trial," *Journal of Affective Disorders* 212 (April 2017): 64–72, doi:10.1016/j.jad.2017.01.028.

12. David A. Jobes, *Managing Suicidal Risk: A Collaborative Approach*, 2nd ed. (New York: Guilford Press, 2016).

11. Suicide Grief, Support, and Healing

1. Junietta Baker McCall, *Bereavement Counseling: Pastoral Care for Complicated Grieving* (Binghamton, NY: Hayworth Press, 2004).

2. "Seeking Help and Support for Grief and Loss," American Cancer Society, last revised May 10, 2019, https://www.cancer.org/treatment/end-of-life-care/grief-and-loss/depression-and-complicated-grief.html.

3. Maurizio Pompili, Amresh Shrivastava, Gianluca Serafini, Marco Innamorati, Mariantonietta Milelli, Denise Erbuto, Frederica Ricci, Dorian A. Lamis, Paolo Scocco, Mario Amore, David Lester, and Paolo Firardi, "Bereavement after the Suicide of a Significant Other," *Indian Journal of Psychiatry* 55, no. 3 (July 2013): 256, doi:10.4103/0019-5545.117145.

4. Pompili et al., "Bereavement after Suicide."

5. Ilanit Tai Young, Alana Iglewicz, Danielle Glorioso, Nicole Lanouette, Kathryn Seay, Manjusha Llapakurti, and Sidney Zisook, "Suicide Bereavement and Complicated Grief," *Dialogues in Clinical Neuroscience* 14, no. 2 (2012): 177–86, https://www.ncbi.nlm.nih.gov/pmc/articles/PMC3384446.

6. Natalie C. Hung and Laura A. Rabin, "Comprehending Childhood Bereavement by Parental Suicide: A Critical Review of Research on Outcomes, Grief Processes, and Interventions," *Death Studies* 3, no. 9 (2009): 781–814, doi:10.1080/07481180903142357.

7. Centre for Addiction and Mental Health, *Hope and Healing after Suicide: A Practical Guide for People Who Have Lost Someone to Suicide in Toronto* (Toronto: Centre for Addiction and Mental Health, 2011), https://www.camh.ca/-/media/files/guides-and-publications/hope-and-healing-en.pdf.

12. Posttraumatic Growth after Suicide

1. Julie Cerel, Myfanwy Maple, Judy van de Venne, Melinda Moore, Chris Flaherty, and Margaret Brown, "Exposure to Suicide in the Community: Prevalence and Correlates in One U.S. State," *Public Health Reports* 131, no. 1 (January–February 2016): doi:10.1177/003335491613100116.

2. Julie Cerel, John McIntosh, Robert A. Neimeyer, Myfanwy Maple, and Doreen S. Marshall, "The Continuum of Survivorship: Definitional Issues in the Aftermath of Suicide," *Suicide and Life-Threatening Behavior* 44, no. 6 (2014): 591–600.

3. Julie Cerel, "We Are All Connected in Suicidology: The Continuum of 'Survivorship'" (plenary presentation, 48th Annual Conference of the American Association of Suicidology, Atlanta, GA, April 18, 2015).

4. Alexandra L. Pitman, David P. J. Osborn, Khadija Rantell, and Michael B. King, "Bereavement by Suicide as a Risk Factor for Suicide Attempt: A Cross-Sectional National UK-Wide Study of 3432 Young Bereaved Adults," *BMJ Open* 6, no. 1 (January 2016): e009948, doi:10.1136/bmjopen-2015-009948.

5. Julie Cerel, Margaret M. Brown, Myfanwy Maple, Michael Singleton, Judy van de Venne, Melinda Moore, and Chris Flaherty, "How Many People Are Exposed to Suicide? Not Six," *Suicide and Life-Threatening Behavior* 49, no. 2 (April 2019): 529–34, doi:10.1111/sltb.12450.

6. Amy E. Latham and Holly G. Prigerson, "Suicidality and Bereavement: Complicated Grief as Psychiatric Disorder Presenting Greatest Risk for Suicidality," *Suicide and Life-Threatening Behavior* 34, no. 4 (2004): 350–62, doi.org/10.1521/suli.34.4.350.53737.

7. Ann M. Mitchell, Yookyung Kim, Holly G. Prigerson, and MaryKay Mortimer-Stephens, "Complicated Grief in Survivors of Suicide," *Crisis* 25, no. 1 (2004): 12–18, doi:10.1027/0227-5910.25.1.12.

8. Faith Communities Task Force, *Suicide Prevention Competencies for Faith Leaders: Supporting Life Before, During, and After a Suicidal Crisis* (Washington, DC: Education Development Center, 2019).

9. Lawrence G. Calhoun and Richard Tedeschi, *Handbook of Posttraumatic Growth: Research and Practice* (New York: Erlbaum, 2006).

10. Lawrence G. Calhoun and Richard G. Tedeschi, "The Foundations of Posttraumatic Growth: New Considerations," *Psychological Inquiry* 15, no. 1 (2004): 93–102, doi.org/10.1207/s15327965pli1501_03.

11. Melinda Moore, Julie Cerel, and David A. Jobes, "Fruits of Trauma? Posttraumatic Growth among Suicide-Bereaved Parents," *Crisis: The Journal of Crisis Intervention and Suicide Prevention* 36, no. 4 (July 2015): 241–48, doi:10.1027/0227-5910/a000318.

12. Melinda M. Moore, Judy van de Venne, and Julie Cerel, "Meaningful Connections of Loss: Posttraumatic Growth in a Sample of Military Veterans, Community Members, and Family Members Exposed and Bereaved by Suicide" (paper presented at the American Association of Suicidology, Atlanta, GA, April 18, 2015).

13. Melinda M. Moore, J. Palmer, and Julie Cerel, "Growth and Hope after Loss: How TAPS Facilitates Posttraumatic Growth in Those Grieving Military Deaths" (report to Tragedy Assistance Program for Survivors, Washington, DC, October 8, 2018).

14. Lawrence G. Calhoun and Richard G. Tedeschi, *Posttraumatic Growth in Clinical Practice* (New York: Routledge, 2013).

15. Calhoun and Tedeschi, "Foundations of Posttraumatic Growth" 15, 93102 doi.org/10.1207/s15327965pli1501_03

16. Michael White, *Maps of Narrative Practice* (New York: W. W. Norton, 2007).

17. E. Betsy Ross, *After Suicide: A Ray of Hope for Those Left Behind* (Cambridge, MA: Perseus, 1997).

13. A Responsive Catholic Community Includes Mental Health Ministry

1. "Hope and Healing: A Pastoral Letter from the Bishops of California on Caring for Those Who Suffer from Mental Illness Addressed to All Catholics and People of Goodwill," California Catholic Conference, May 1, 2018, https://www.caCatholic.org/hope_and_healing.

2. Wendell J. Callahan, Liberty Hebron, and Alissa N. Willmerdinger, *Catholic Mental Health Ministry: Guidelines for Implementation* (San Diego: University of San Diego, 2019).

3. Christopher G. Ellison, Margaret L. Vaaler, Kevin J. Flannelly, and Andrew J. Weaver, "The Clergy as a Source of Mental Health Assistance: What Americans Believe," *Review of Religious Research* 48, no. 2 (December 2006): 190–211.

4. Lee Michael Williams, "The Impact of Mental Illness on Spouses and Family Members (conference session, the University of San Diego Catholic Institute for Mental Health Ministry, San Diego, CA, February 23, 2019).

5. Mark D. Underwood and Victoria Arango, "Evidence for Neurodegeneration and Neuroplasticity as Part of the Neurobiology of Suicide," *Biological Psychiatry* 70, no. 4 (August 2011): 306–7; Mark D. Underwood, Suham A. Kassir, Mihran J. Bakalian, Hanga Galfalvy, Andrew J. Dwork, J. John Mann, and Victoria Arango, "Serotonin Receptors and Suicide, Major Depression, Alcohol Use Disorder and Reported Early Life Adversity," *Translational Psychiatry* 8, no. 1 (December 2018): 279; Stefano Puglisi-Allegra and Diego Andolina, "Serotonin and Stress Coping," *Behavioural Brain Research* 277 (2015): 58–67.

6. Underwood et al., "Serotonin Receptors and Suicide," 279.

7. "Mental Health by the Numbers," National Alliance on Mental Illness, last modified September 2019, https://www.nami.org/learn-more/mental-health-by-the-numbers.

8. Jean Vanier and John Swinton, *Mental Health: The Inclusive Church Resource* (London: Darton, Longman and Todd, 2014).

9. Greg Boyle (keynote address, the annual conference of the Juvenile Court, Community and Alternative School Administrators of California, May 2006, San Diego, CA).

10. "Mental Health Myth and Facts," MentalHealth.gov, last modified August 29, 2017, https://www.mentalhealth.gov/basics/mental-health-myths-facts.

11. "What Is Mental Health First Aid?" Mental Health First Aid, accessed July 30, 2018, https://www.mentalhealthfirstaid.org/faq.

14. Loving Outreach to Survivors of Suicide

1. *America* magazine featured the LOSS program in the March 19, 2018, edition. The feature described the program in detail, interviewing three survivors who benefited from the program, and outlined the services that survivors can access.

15. Youth Ministry and Suicide

1. Hanna Rosin, *The Atlantic*, December 2015.

2. *ABC News*, February 16, 2016.

3. "The Developmental Assets Framework," Search Institute, accessed January 20, 2020, https://www.search-institute.org/our-research/development-assets/developmental-assets-framework.

4. National Conference of Catholic Bishops, *Renewing the Vision: A Framework for Catholic Youth Ministry* (Washington, DC: USCCB Publishing, 1997).

5. Peter L. Benson, *All Kids Are Our Kids: What Communities Must Do to Raise Caring and Responsible Children and Adolescents*, 2nd ed. (San Francisco: Jossey-Bass, 2006).

6. "The Developmental Relationships Framework," Search Institute, accessed January 20, 2020, https://www.search-institute.org/developmental-relationships/developmental-relationships-framework.

7. Roy Petitfils, *Helping Teens with Stress, Anxiety, and Depression: A Field Guide for Catholic Parents, Pastors, and Youth Leaders* (Notre Dame, IN: Ave Maria Press, 2019).

8. The Dougy Center, *Supporting Children and Teens after a Suicide Death*, accessed January 20, 2020, https://www.dougy.org/docs/TDC_Supporting_Children__Teens_After_a_Suicide_Death_2018.pdf.

The Association of Catholic Mental Health Ministers is a lay association whose members walk with people living with a mental illness and their families to help them find the support and services that they need. ACMHM members work to eliminate the stigma and discrimination that people living with a mental illness encounter in the Church and in the world. Members strive to strengthen mental health ministry in the Catholic Church by networking and sharing resources. www.catholicmhm.org

Ed Shoener was ordained a permanent deacon in 2004 and serves at St. Peter's Cathedral in the Diocese of Scranton. He is a founding member of the Association of Catholic Mental Health Ministers, the Catholic Institute of Mental Health Ministry at the University of San Diego, and the Scranton Mental Health Ministry. He serves on the boards of the Council on Mental Illness, National Catholic Partnership on Disability, and Pathways to Promise. He earned a graduate certificate in spiritual direction from the Aquinas Institute of Theology.

Shoener is president of Shoener Environmental Consulting. He has a bachelor of science degree in environmental research management from Penn State University, where he also earned a master's degree in environmental protection control.

Shoener's family and friends founded the Katie Foundation after his daughter, Kathleen, died by suicide in 2016. The obituary he wrote for her went viral. The Shoeners live in Scranton, Pennsylvania.

catholicmhm.org
thekatiefoundation.org
Facebook: The Katie Foundation

Most Rev. John P. Dolan is auxiliary bishop of San Diego. He also serves the diocese as vicar general, moderator of the curia, and vicar for clergy. Ordained to the priesthood in 1989, Dolan became auxiliary bishop in 2017.

He is the chaplain of the Lost Boys of Sudan, a member of the Catholic Institute for Mental Health Ministry, and a board member of Father Joe's Villages, a ministry to the homeless. Dolan earned his bachelor's degree in philosophy from the University of San Diego and master's degrees in divinity and theology from St. Patrick's Seminary in Menlo Park, California. He is the author of *Rose of Lima: A Nine-Day Study of Her Life* and *Who Is Like God? A Nine-Day Journey with St. Michael.*

www.sdcatholic.org/bishops/auxiliary-bishop-dolan/

Do You Know Someone Who Is Grieving a Loss from Suicide?

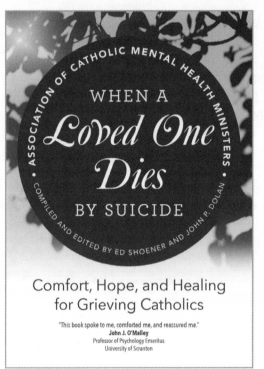

WHEN A
Loved One Dies
BY SUICIDE

ASSOCIATION OF CATHOLIC MENTAL HEALTH MINISTERS

COMPILED AND EDITED BY ED SHOENER AND JOHN P. DOLAN

Comfort, Hope, and Healing
for Grieving Catholics

"This book spoke to me, comforted me, and reassured me."
John J. O'Malley
Professor of Psychology Emeritus
University of Scranton

When a Loved One Dies by Suicide includes the personal stories of Catholics who have lost a loved one to suicide. The authors also share about learni to cope with the crushing grief of finding comfort in faith and community, and of eventually discovering hope as they bega to move forward again. They share their pain, insight, and comfort, along with important information from mental healt experts and Church leaders so that you have the spiritual support you need to find hope and healing.

"This book spoke to me, comforted me, and reassured me."
—John J. O'Malley
Professor of Psychology Emeritus
University of Scranton